Praise for

# WALK ON

"Somehow from the depths of his own despair, Stephen Panus has provided an achingly beautiful guidebook for finding joy and hope."

—Dana O'Neill, author of *The Big East: Inside the Most Entertaining and Influential Conference in College Basketball History* and writer at *The Athletic*

"Stephen Panus suffered through every parent's most horrific nightmare—the loss of a child. I can't imagine the pain associated with such a devastating loss and can only conclude that it's not something you ever get over but only hope to get beyond. Jake Panus will never be forgotten. And his legacy and the mark he left on the world will live on forever. This is a story of unimaginable hurt but inspiration, courage, gratitude, and the reminder to always be present and live in the moment. This is a must-read and an instant classic. *Walk On* is a courageous and brilliant work."

—Jim Rome, CBS Sports Radio/CBS Sports

"As a university president, I was all too frequently called on to share the grief of families and friends of a student who was lost to the world. While there is little that can soften the pain in the short term, this book offers promise and hope, like rays of the sun, through grieving. The promise and hope of Panus's words are an inspiration. I hope that they might reach all who are facing the need to cope with personal tragedy."

>—Harris Pastides, president emeritus at University of South Carolina

"Stephen Panus is an inspiration. It's impossible to understand the pain of losing a child. Stephen manages to bring you along with him as he beautifully shares his love for his son Jake and his ability to turn the deepest pain into smiles and tears of joy for others. Through his words in this mesmerizing and beautifully written book on finding a path through the devastation and unrelenting pain of losing a child, he transforms his ever-present sadness to make a true difference in the lives of young men and women in his son's name. Jake Panus is watching with pride, as his legacy burns brighter through his father's love."

>—Mark Hilinski, cofounder of Hilinski's Hope with his wife, Kym, and father to Kelly, Tyler, and Ryan

"With *Walk On*, Stephen Panus shares with shocking detail a father's palpable sorrow in the aftermath of the tragic loss of a son. You feel the weight of the journey toward peace in every word. The honesty in these pages offers simultaneously an injection of perspective for the simplicity of life's truest joys and a refuge for grief-stricken people that they are not alone."

>—Marty Smith, ESPN reporter, *New York Times* best-selling author

"This is a brave and beautifully written book about unbearable loss and a father's never-ending battle to honor a son, comfort a family, and make the world a better place."

—Joe Drape, *New York Times* bestselling author of *Soldiers First: Duty, Honor, Country and Football at West Point*

"There is no question *Walk On* will change lives. Stephen Panus's vulnerability relating his experience as a parent who has suffered the most tragic loss is shocking and transformative. His storytelling about navigating a new normal you wouldn't wish on your worst enemy grabs you by the collar. I cried at the gut-wrenching personal descriptions and also am incredibly inspired by the lessons Stephen shares as tools and suggestions for all of us to make the most of the time we have and the people who matter most in our lives. His messages that began as Post-Its to his children are observations and lessons I hope to pass onto my own kids."

—Lindsay Czarniak, Fox Sports

"Stephen Panus has done something incredible. He has written a book about a tragedy that will inspire and fill you with hope. Hug your loved ones, then read *Walk On* to remind you why you're doing it. I'm so grateful I did."

—Kyle Brandt, NFL Network, CBS Sports

"It's all here: the body blow, the pain, the fury, the helplessness of watching your family in pain, the questions about God, the questions about your own life, the sense of meaninglessness, and again and again, the pain. But an antidote is here, too: the transformation of love into purpose. Panus writes with intensity and clarity about his son's death and how, with time, his own grief eases and changes, but his love stays fixed."

 —Ann Finkbeiner, freelance science writer; author of *After the Death of a Child*

"Stephen Panus pulls us through the journey of every parent's worst nightmare with visceral storytelling and inspirational lessons. Emotion and inspiration swell from the page. Parent or not, *Walk On* is a must-read."

 —Rob Marciano, senior meteorologist, ABC's *World News Tonight* and *Good Morning America*

"Anyone who has ever lost a child joins a club they never wanted to be a part of. Then they get a choice: to languish in the pain or find the best way to honor the child they'll forever miss. Stephen chose the latter and has done so in an inspiring way. It's the story of his path forward and a guide for others still trying to find the light."

 —Kenny Mayne

"From unimaginable tragedy to unrelenting inspiration, Stephen Panus walks us through the journey no parent would ever want and then never allows us to wallow in it. The passing of his son, Jake, is not an anchor that brings us down but a buoy that helps us float. Jake's story will live on thanks to Stephen's poignant telling. And maybe there is a playbook for any parent facing a similarly trying situation. *Walk On* is incredible."

 —Ian Rapoport, NFL Network Insider

"This is a heartbreaking and powerfully raw testimony to the strength of the human spirit and the everlasting bond of a parent to their child. I cannot imagine a world without my child in it. Stephen gives us an unflinching glimpse at what that world looks like and shows us the incredible strength and perseverance it takes to *Walk On*."

—Monti Carlo, food TV personality

"Stephen's experience should be a lesson for us all. Life may confront us with seemingly overwhelming obstacles and unimaginable grief, but in those times when we are seemingly at our weakest, our strength and faith are stronger than we could ever imagine. It's how you emerge from tragedy that helps define you. And that's what Stephen courageously demonstrates to all of us in *Walk On*."

—Chris Fallica, Fox Sports

"Stephen Panus brings us closer to his story of devastating loss and heartbreak to create a guiding light toward hope and restoration. No matter the challenges you face in life, this book will help you reframe your mindset and bring you closer to the life you were meant to lead with great intent and purpose."

—Lauren Sisler, ESPN sports reporter and inspirational speaker

"I don't win many wagers, but the bet I'm making on this book—detailing how Stephen Panus and his family are coping with an unspeakable loss—being a success is a guaranteed lock."

—Cousin Sal Iacono, Emmy award-winning writer, television personality, and cofounder of *The Extra Points* podcast network

"*Walk On* is a beautiful journey of resilience and depiction that even after our darkest moments, we can use those tragedies to provide hope and opportunity for the future."

> —Jennifer King, assistant running backs coach, Washington Commanders

"After the tragic death of his son, Jake, Stephen Panus has somehow used the tragedy to gift the world with life lessons that you need to stop and digest now. Do not walk off without *Walk On* in your hand."

> —Darren Rovell, sports business reporter

"Stephen Panus takes us on a very emotional and inspirational ride. *Walk On* teaches us what true adversity is and how to fight on and live your best life after unimaginable loss. This book gives us an amazing perspective of what's really important in life."

> —Mike Repole, food and beverage entrepreneur

"Writing with the emotional heartbeat of a parent who has suffered great loss and yet determined to share inspirational perseverance, Stephen Panus's *Walk On* is a story that grips your soul and forces you to feel deeply. The ability to turn the ultimate loss into a strong motivational impact reveals Stephen's courage, faith, and resolve. It is a brilliantly delivered lesson in love and hope. And Jake is proud."

> —Holly Cain, veteran sports journalist and author

"What we call chicken skin in Hawaii is better known to most simply as goosebumps. Either way, it's the reaction one gets to a powerful, emotional stimulus. *Walk On* delivers such a feeling from Stephen Panus's first words—that first picture he presents of the son he lost and what he eventually gained from that loss. A beautifully written story about something so personally debilitating. Jake's spirit lives in the words, in the pictures, and in the goodwill his death prompted."

—Neil Everett

"A heartbreaking story of an unbearable, unexpected loss. Father, brother, and mother find faith and meaning in the uncertainty of life. We must enjoy and realize every moment is a gift from God."

—Doug O'Neill, two-time Kentucky Derby-winning Thoroughbred trainer

*Walk On*

by Stephen Panus

© Copyright 2024 Stephen Panus

ISBN 979-8-88824-295-7

All rights reserved. No part of this publication may be reproduced, stored in a retrieval system, or transmitted in any form or by any means—electronic, mechanical, photocopy, recording, or any other—except for brief quotations in printed reviews, without the prior written permission of the author.

Published by

3705 Shore Drive
Virginia Beach, VA 23455
800-435-4811
www.koehlerbooks.com

# WALK ON

## STEPHEN PANUS

VIRGINIA BEACH
CAPE CHARLES

Jake, March 2020

# Dedication

THIS BOOK IS dedicated to my son, Liam, who lost a lifetime with his best friend and older brother, Jake.

> "My heart shattered, broken into millions of pieces,
> The day you died.
> And because there was nothing else to do,
> I let those shattered pieces land softly in the world.
> And when I could, again, breathe, with a regular rhythm,
> I noticed—quietly, painfully—the places
> where splintered shards of my heart came to a rest.
> Somewhere amidst the fragments of your too-brief-life,
> reflecting ineluctable grief,
> I know that your love is, by comparison,
> so much more vast and infinite than my shattering."
>
> —Dr. Joanne Cacciatore, *Bearing the Unbearable*
> © 2013, 2017 All Rights Reserved

# Table of Contents

Preface .................................................................... 1

The Most Painful Goodbye ................................... 4

Motion with Meaning Leads to Living with Purpose ............ 29

Be Relentless with Your Effort as Your Attitude
    Determines Your Altitude .................................... 34

Care to Serve & Dare to Be Kind ........................... 40

Have the Courage to Be Yourself ........................... 46

Character Is Just as Important as Talent ................ 52

The Magnitude of Gratitude ................................ 57

Accountability: Your Choices = Your Consequences ... 63

Realize Your Resolve & Discover Your Genuineness ... 72

Change Is the Only Constant ................................ 78

Most People Never Run Far Enough/
    Your Determination Will Define You .................. 81

The Little Things Are the Big Things ..................... 88

Power of Hope/No Mud on the Brain .................... 97

Don't Fumble Your Honesty & Humility ................ 101

Outside Perspective Leads to Inner Reflection ....... 106

Be it. Don't Talk it. ............................................. 116

Live Your Life in Harmony ................................... 122

Look Life in the Face ............................................................ 125

Be Hungry for the Experience in Your Journey ................ 129

The Pursuit of Happiness ..................................................... 134

Be Great Together ................................................................. 138

Enthusiasm Is Contagious .................................................... 141

Family Ties/Friendships Matter .......................................... 144

Two Ears, One Mouth ........................................................... 149

Forgiveness Is Healing .......................................................... 152

Epilogue .................................................................................. 157

Acknowledgments ................................................................. 161

# Preface

by Shane Beamer,

Head Football Coach, University of South Carolina

THE NIGHT OF December 5, 2020, was a dream come true for me. After twenty-one years in coaching, I was offered the position of head football coach at the University of South Carolina by Ray Tanner, our athletic director.

At this time, I was coaching at the University of Oklahoma, but I had previously spent 2007 to 2010 coaching at the University of South Carolina. I loved my time in Columbia, South Carolina, and for ten years, had wanted nothing more than the opportunity to return.

That night and the two weeks after Coach Tanner called me were a blur. My wife, three children, and I had a special family embrace celebrating the news. We cried tears of joy. The next several weeks were nonstop. There were so many things to do. Meeting the team, recruiting new players, hiring a coaching staff, and finding somewhere to live were just a few of the things that occupied my time.

I will never forget the wake-up call that month about what's really important. I received a phone call about a huge South Carolina Gamecock fan dealing with an unspeakable tragedy, the loss of a child. I was told that a phone call from me, the new head football coach at South Carolina, could hopefully lift his spirits during an extremely dark time.

That was the first time I ever heard the name "Stephen Panus." I will never forget sitting in my house in Norman, Oklahoma, talking to Stephen for the first time. The pain in his voice and the hurt in his heart over the loss of his son, Jake, came through the phone loud and clear. I was stressing about a new job and all it entails while listening to someone dealing with something so much deeper and much more important.

I knew, after talking on the phone, that there was something special and different about Stephen. I was blown away by his resolve and quiet strength in a dark time. I know he would be determined to turn a devastating tragedy into something positive. I also knew I wanted to help.

I am humbled to play a small part in the development of the Jake Panus Walk On Scholarship. This annual scholarship goes to a member of our football team who embodies so many of the characteristics that Jake did. It's always an emotional day when Stephen presents this to one of our players. I know our players love hearing about Jake and all the things that made him special.

Our team has 120 players on it. We have eighty-five players on scholarship and thirty-five who pay their own tuition for the opportunity to be a member of our team. Those are our walk-ons. Each one of them is a true member of and an asset to our team. They make our team better. There is no doubt in my mind that Jake Panus would have made our team better had he been on it.

I have learned a lot about Jake from talking to Stephen. I learned even more about him from reading this book. Stephen says, "Each act of kindness creates a ripple, and the echoes of kindness are endless." That embodies Jake Panus. It is evident that Jake had a strong passion and desire for lifting people up.

We have core values in our program; these core values are what we want to be about. Jake lived his life embodying so many of our core values. Gratitude, positive energy, and accountability are just a few. Stephen will illustrate why these values and others can help you live a more productive and joyful life.

I am grateful for all I have learned from Stephen over the last three years. I am constantly amazed by him. Stephen states that life is about determining who you want in your foxhole. Who do you want in your locker room? There is no doubt that I would have wanted Jake Panus in mine with me!

I have used the expression "Find some joy" many times—trying to see things with a positive mindset, a glass-half-full perspective. Stephen and his family suffered an unimaginable tragedy, but they have not let that event be the end. Despite their pain, they have managed to bring joy to so many, whether it be through the Jake Panus Walk On Scholarship, their son Liam deciding to live his life more like Jake, or just simple, thoughtful texts to a guy like me.

Jake Panus brought joy to so many people. His life with us was cut way too short, but his impact is still felt and will continue to be. Jake's light continues to shine!

# The Most Painful Goodbye

*"I wish I could show you . . .
the astonishing light of your own being."*

—Hafez

IT WAS A warm summer Sunday in early August 2020. My wife, Kellie, and I had just completed a fifteen-mile bike ride along the southern coastline of Connecticut. We were energized and, having returned home, in the midst of preparing our next excursion—a trip to the weekly local farmer's market to gather some freshly nurtured vegetables to grill for dinner. Then Kellie's phone rang. There had been an accident, we were informed, and our elder son, Jake, age sixteen, was injured. That's all the details we were provided.

Two days prior, Jake joined his girlfriend and her mother and brother for a long, quiet family weekend getaway to Block Island (a tiny straight of rocky land and sandy beaches, a popular summertime destination nestled in the Atlantic Ocean just off the coast of Rhode Island). This was his first girlfriend (they had only been dating for about six weeks) and his first time going away with her family. The trip, as proposed, would be replete with beach time, board games, ice cream, walks to town, and cookouts. Safe family fun was what Jake's girlfriend's mother promised us. "I will be watching all the kids, so not to worry"—the final words the mother texted Kellie. We entrusted the care of our son to that mother. Two days later, her call to Kellie changed everything.

Frantic and without answers, Kellie hastily packed a bag of overnight necessities as I grabbed our youngest son, Liam, eleven years old at the time, and we all sprinted to the driveway and hopped into our car. I sped us toward Rhode Island, a two-hour trip from our home in Connecticut along the I-95 corridor. Kellie desperately dialed 911 in Rhode Island, and they confirmed a car crash but had no other details. I gripped the wheel and drove as fast as I could, weaving around cars and bouncing between lanes. Liam, nervous and confused, sat squarely in the middle of the front edge of the rear seat, hunched over and falling forward into the middle console between us. Then Kellie's phone rang again, this time with a 401 area code. We were a mere twelve minutes into the drive, speeding toward Rhode Island. Kellie answered it with the speaker on.

It was the most unwanted phone call ever. On the other line was a doctor, who hesitated for a second before uttering, "I'm sorry . . . but I just pronounced your son dead." Kellie screamed the most primal, guttural sound I had ever heard. It was savage-like, fierce, and categorically heart-wrenching. My heart and head exploded. Liam burst into tears and fell flat into the middle console.

I slowly steered the vehicle toward the right lane, wailing unrecognizable words and sounds. Everything was moving in slow motion. At the first available exit, I darted off the highway, driving straight into a vacant bank parking lot, where I slammed the car into park. We opened our doors and ran circles around the car toward each other before involuntarily descending to the worn pavement as one blob of broken humanity, showering each other with uncontrollable tears. In an instant, we were overtaken by the most immediate, intense pain. The doctor was still on the line, waiting for us to safely exit the highway as Kellie clutched her phone in her right hand.

The attending physician's words hung in the air like a summertime convective cloud. Everything went black. I couldn't hear another word he uttered. I was numb. My life had abruptly and indelibly imploded. We sat, stood, kicked, shook, and screamed at the sky, completely immersed in a level of trauma I wouldn't wish upon any soul.

There are losses that indelibly alter your life and upend how you view the universe. Losing Jake was just that for me and my family. It was soul-crushing. Our hearts weren't just cracked and broken, rather it was as if a hand reached inside each of us and ripped out our beating hearts. A parent's worst nightmare instantly became our reality.

Later that Sunday evening, the details of Jake's death surfaced: He was a passenger in a vehicle that was operated recklessly and went off the road. The driver was arrested on multiple charges, including driving under the influence. The driver . . . was Jake's teenage girlfriend. Despite her reassurances and promise to watch over the children, the mother, who was the only adult on the trip, had failed us. In fact, it was later learned that she handed the car's keys to her daughter, who had been drinking. She stuffed six other teenage children into her SUV and sent them on their way. Little did we know that there had been much to worry about.

As the minutes turned into hours and days evolved into weeks, it felt as if aliens had abducted Jake. One minute, Jake was here, joyfully with us, and then, poof, at the snap of our fingers, he was gone. His luggage returned, but he did not. His girlfriend and friends returned, but not Jake. His junior year of high school commenced for all his classmates, but not for Jake. His room sat eerily empty and quiet, everything untouched, just the way he left it. His luggage from that fateful trip eventually arrived home, remaining sealed and buried deep in a closet.

Adding to the surrealness of this tragedy are Jake's haunting, final words. Forty-eight hours prior to the crash, our entire family huddled in our pajamas outside on our mudroom porch on a very early, humid Friday morning to see Jake off. Mere seconds before his girlfriend, one year older than Jake, arrived to pick him up, Jake looked at all of us, smiled, and nonchalantly said, *"You guys are acting like you will never see me again."* He then hugged each of us goodbye, strolled, luggage in tow, down the driveway, turned back around, and flashed a brilliant smile and his signature peace sign before hopping into his girlfriend's awaiting car. They backed out of our driveway and sped away. That was the last time I saw Jake alive, felt his bear hug, and heard the final words I would hear him speak.

Jake was an immense, magnetic personality who lived his life lifting up others. He was authentic in every sense of the word and welcomed everyone with an infectious smile. He sought joy in everything he did as if it was air—vital to his existence. His charisma, supreme confidence, and compassion emerged early in his formative years. He was both an old soul and an über-social being. He was the life of any gathering, whether in the classroom or on the athletic field. Jake simply made anywhere he was better, brighter, more fun, and happier.

He was a rising star with a gravitational pull stronger than Jupiter and was adored by and attracted a circle of friends from coast to coast. From an early age, Jake was confident conversing with adults in ways beyond his years. His friend group spanned generations, and his empathy and humanity welcomed all. He was caring, capable of relating to others' joys and pains, and always there to help or listen with an optimistic ear for those who needed it the most.

There were no boundaries to Jake's adventure and living life to its fullest. When he learned he was going to be a big brother as he approached his fifth birthday, he jumped for joy, bounding across the sofa, arms raised in victory, bellowing screams of ecstasy. He adored his little brother and cherished their brotherhood and his role as the older brother and protector.

As days and nights blurred into weeks and months, the shock and relentless trauma evolved into profound sorrow, merciless pain, and ceaseless grief. I didn't just breathe in oxygen every day. In addition, every new inhale included grief. Omnipresent in my new world, I struggled to recall what life was like without grief. There was life with Jake—and now this life where I had no choice but to live and move forward without him. Yet moving forward proved challenging. Those memories of joyful, more lighthearted times seemed distant—a galaxy away.

Grief is far from a linear pathway and instead lays itself out like an unwelcome maze of intertwined, arduous hiking routes leading steeply up a jagged rockface. I awake every morning as if being asked to climb my own personal Mt. Kilimanjaro. And surrendering is no easy task. The invisible backpack I carry seemingly gets heavier with each day. Moreover, part of me yearns not to move another day further away from that apocalyptic Sunday in August of 2020, as it only serves to create even more distance between me and what I lost. Yet, I'm told and often encouraged that each passing day is a step toward healing. However, this isn't a broken back or an injury or adversity with a timeline returning me to a full recovery. I don't subscribe to the theory that a complete recovery is ever possible from acute grief and trauma from suddenly losing a child. Rather, it's a total disorientation of the mind as the remaining years of my life will now forever be weighed down by this loss. I realize I will never, ever, be completely whole again or the same person I once was. My life is split into a two-act play.

To this day, a part of my brain still finds it challenging to truly embrace and accept the realization that I will never see Jake, my beloved, authentic, beautiful, and charismatic sixteen-year-old son, again. I stare out the kitchen window, longing to see him cutting across the library grass from the other side of the street, strutting down our driveway toward me with his bright smile and golden locks, mostly covered with his baseball cap turned backward. Occasionally, I open his dresser drawers, lift an article of clothing to my nose, and inhale his aroma before quickly returning it to the drawer and sealing it tightly in fear of one day losing his scent.

He was mere months into his sixteenth year on the planet and possessed such a bright future. Now, he's eternally a child. The final photographic images I have of Jake are cemented in time. I will never see him evolve past that beautiful sixteen-year-old pose. He was just on the precipice of becoming a man, developing those chiseled cheekbones and embracing his drop-dead gorgeous blond curls that were the envy of women and men alike. Instead, it simply was the un-sweetest sixteenth year ever.

No matter what I have attempted to return to or even seek out, it's there, hanging, like a cloud of dust, not dissimilar from the character Pigpen in the comic series "Peanuts." The major distinction was that Pigpen's cloud of dust was clearly visible to one and all. In the case of profound grief, the personal cloud of dust is invisible to all but the griever. On the outside, I essentially look the same, only because no one can see my insides, which are twisted, shattered, gutted, and battered. Grief is an ever-present black cloud. It's there when I open my eyes in the morning and strong enough to awaken me in the middle of the night. No matter where I go, so goes the invisible black cloud. Author C. S. Lewis discovered in his own grief, "Part of every misery is, so to speak, the misery's shadow or reflection."

It's been said that a father is supposed to protect his children, and from that, he derives meaning. I certainly honor that I found great meaning in rearing Jake, just as I do with Liam. Like many fathers, I certainly felt a responsibility to protect my sons. However, protecting them is a mirage. We allow our children to go places without us by their side, like school, sleepaway camps, field trips, sporting events, and weekend getaways, without batting an eye, until that perception of control is shattered into a million pieces. When that happens, the first person you blame is yourself. The game of what-ifs begins in earnest, sending your mind racing down a zillion pathways that all conclude at the same dead-end reality. Your child is dead, and there wasn't a damn thing you could have done to prevent it—unless, of course, you placed your child in a bubble and never allowed him to leave the house.

Contrary to any assertion otherwise, time does not heal. Rather, it tricks the mind as months turn into years, making people who are no longer present feel as if they were never present. The gaping wound remains no matter how much time passes. It's a life sentence of the first noble truth of Buddhism (life is suffering) served in a super-sized portion. I had invested so much of myself, everything, in fact, into raising this beautiful boy and kind soul. And now there appeared to be absolutely nothing, zilch, to show for it.

It's unnatural and out of the natural order of life to lose a child, thus making the new me a misfit in society, equally out of order and without any known remedy or available repair—struggling to find new meaning or purpose as the daily ebb and flow of life swiftly came and went. A part of me died that day with Jake, as did a part of his mother and brother. We're all very different from who we were prior to August 9, 2020. Liam didn't just lose a brother; he lost parts of his mother and father—a trifecta of tragedy. Kellie lost her faith in everything, most especially in God.

It was a struggle to see my wife in such agony. I was helpless, incapable of changing these harsh and savage circumstances. There simply was nothing I could do or say to alleviate her grief or mine. All I can do is support and love her. The collateral damage that ensues from the sudden loss of a child has far-reaching, lasting implications. The reverberations ripple out like a nuclear bomb explosion (think Chernobyl) and impact every facet of your life. Everything changes. The darkness of grief is enveloping. Admittedly, there were times of such profound darkness that each of us experienced feelings of not wanting to live anymore. There is no escape from the grief of suddenly losing a child so young. Like love, it's everlasting.

Grief is an unwelcome topic in our society because it carries a stigma like none other. It's not just that it feels like a foreign emotion, but it also scares the living shit out of people. Few can be comfortably close to death or grief. Losing a child tops a parent's worst nightmare list, so it only makes sense that parents do not want to get too close to it. Yet grief is all around us. While my brain tells me I'm not alone, it often feels that way in my heart. But a simple Google search reveals children are dying, sadly, every day—whether from accidents, illness, disease, suicide, gun violence, or otherwise.

In time (much time), I resolved that Jake's passing can never be fixed, altered, or even logically accepted by my brain. Instead, it can only be carried forward and honored. But how does one reenter life and move forward when your heart is cracked open into a million pieces? How does one accept such a blow, stay standing, and tote such a heavy loss?

The timing and answers are different for everyone. Grief is an individual journey, no different than falling in love with someone. While there is comfort in the collective mourning with family and friends, everyone's path is distinctly their own. Undoubtedly, we each need support in grief, but the trek toward accepting or being able to fill the cracks of one's heart with light instead of pain is a solitary one. And what I have come to genuinely embrace is that the intensity of my grief over losing Jake unabashedly matched the intensity of my unconditional love for my son.

Despite the ferocity of the torture we suffered, Kellie and

I remained committed to ensuring our family would endure. We were warned that many marriages dissolve because of such an epic, life-changing loss. Our unflinching, unconditional love and support for each other ultimately served as an unbreakable commitment and bond. We would weather this storm together and emerge, somehow, still standing and capable of walking onward. We clung to and supported one another through debilitating ups and downs, over rough days and weeks, during unique triggering events, and amid showers of tears and rage at our life circumstances and fate.

I devoured book after book, searching for the meaning of life and grappling with not just understanding my grief but seeking meaning beyond it. I wanted to know how the hell I was supposed to come out of this in any recognizable and functional way. How did others survive such pain from their own life-changing events? I found inspiration from some who were dealt their own absolute hell and crawled, scraped, and climbed up the mountain again. From others, I extracted lessons in the essence of humanity and what truly matters, as well as their thoughts on the meaning of life and what may or may not happen to us in the next realm.

I desperately searched for answers. It's how our brains are wired. We need to understand. How and why this happened to us topped the list. Yet those answers will never be provided in this lifetime. Fathers who also lost children reached out and offered an available ear, wisdom, their experiences, and, perhaps most importantly, comfort at my lowest point. Many told me how other fathers had reached out to them in the wake of their tragedies, and they, in turn, felt an obligation to do the same for me—humanity at its best during its worst.

In the days following the crash, we received a beautiful handwritten letter from a ninety-seven-year-old gentleman who lived a mere three-minute drive from our home. In his letter, he penned the pertinent details of his prodigious life story, revealed his empathy, and concluded with an olive branch of hope. He wrote how, over fifty years ago, he lost two of his six children in the span of months. Both children died in horrific, tragic car accidents, the toll of which ultimately ended his first marriage. We read and reread the letter, wondering who this man was. We soon learned that he had remarried a lovely woman, who, it turned out, had been a yoga student of Kellie's. Yet we had never had occasion to meet him . . . until now.

Several weeks after we received his letter, his wife asked Kellie if he could come and visit with us. We welcomed him with broken hearts and open arms. He gingerly exited his car and, with the assistance of a cane, maneuvered down our driveway and over a bridge spanning a small stream that runs through our property. We sat outside by our firepit and amongst nature on an early, sunny fall afternoon. I listened intently as he gently spoke, elegantly selecting his words with precision and compassion. I watched as tears slowly dripped from his eyes and dribbled down his cheeks as he teleported back to his own trauma. His pain, despite all those passing years, was not just palpable; it was visible. Our fresh pain and grief had awoken his own in the most reflective manner. He was wise and learned and had his heart ripped out (twice) like no human being should ever experience. Despite the torment and sorrow, he had found a way to move forward and had lived a rich and fulfilling life. Yet here he was, kindly offering us the remaining remnants of his heart, along with his foresight and ear, imparting his reassurance and comforting us at our darkest hours.

Subsequently, we visited with him and his wife several times at their home. To say he lived a full life is an understatement. Despite the significant adversity he confronted, he never stopped moving forward. After graduating from Yale Law School, he helped found a successful law office, where he worked well into his nineties. Prior to that, he attended Dartmouth in the fall of 1942, leaving after one semester to join the Army and serve during World War II. For more than two years, he was part of the US Army Infantry 273rd Regiment, serving in the United Kingdom, Belgium, France, and Germany and earning the Expert and Combat Infantry badges and the Bronze Star. He was an avid sportsman; he fished for trout from Patagonia to Labrador and from New Zealand to France. He traveled the globe, volunteered his time, and shared his intellect and compassion amongst a range of civic, academic, and philanthropic ventures. His initial letter spawned an amazing, yet short-lived friendship between us. Months later, he passed quietly at his home surrounded by family.

There is a community, sadly, of us. We are the unnamed—bereaved parents who have lost children for one reason or another. And we intimately understand each other's plight and pain. We quietly carry this grief and understand that some days the waves of grief can feel overwhelming, set off by what appears to others to be a non-consequential, everyday occurrence. Yet for us, landmines and pitfalls exist everywhere, no matter how much time has elapsed. Whether it's a song on the radio, an aroma from the kitchen, a trip to the grocery store, or driving by the high school, triggers are everywhere, cocked and loaded, just waiting for us. So, we tread this earth carefully. Our eyes may appear wide open, and our outward appearance may reveal little, but we dodge and weave our way slowly forward through each day, protecting the remaining remnants of our broken yet still beating hearts.

There is no shame in grief or opening your heart to the painful emotions provoked by it. Here's the truth: *our vulnerability is our strength.* Inside the heavy-heartedness and fluid reflux of lachrymose, you will find yourself capable of gripping, bearing, and simply being with these agonizing feelings. In doing so, I began to identify with a heart of love and compassion as part of my coping process, allowing me to feel and relate to the deepest pain and suffering in others.

Now, when I read about or hear of other children dying, no matter the reason, my heart immediately does two things: 1) it triggers a brisk teleport of my soul right back to August 9, 2020, and 2) it connects me to the pain, sorrow, grief, anguish, and heartbreak that those parents and surviving family must now endure and carry. I ache for them. I sometimes write the parents letters, like others did for me. This club does not need any more new members. I hate writing those letters. There are too many children dying—too many senseless and tragic deaths.

I had always been an optimist, capable of seeing opportunity and hope even under less-than-ideal and challenging times. Yet this life-changing experience of confronting grief and the most primal sense of impermanence on such intimate and painful terms made all previous adversity seem like child's play. Grief crushes optimism and absolutely smothers it. My grief shows itself in a variety of ways. It resides and flows through daily fatigue, stinging knots in my stomach, seemingly oversized lumps in my throat, and aches in my bones before emerging as involuntary tears, spewing out whenever and however they need to. The pain rings differently depending on the day, trigger, or memories that flash before me.

It has taken every ounce of my spirit to lift myself up off the proverbial floor of life. This experience slammed me harder than I've ever been hit. It didn't just knock the wind out of me; it expunged a paramount purpose and shredded my heart. Yet I awoke each day intent on doing whatever was needed to merely survive another day. The mantra "one day at a time" took on new meaning. I found gratitude for my inner fortitude, which refused to allow me to be entirely swallowed up by the magnitude of this darkness. No matter how somber things appeared and how much dead weight I became, I clung to faith and threads of hope.

Helen Keller, ever the optimist, once shared, "Although the world is full of suffering, it is full also of the overcoming of it."

*Okay*, I thought, recalling the line from *Dumb and Dumber*, "So you're telling me there's a chance." *But how*, I kept asking myself, *can I overcome such a crippling invasion and abduction within our family?* Months later, I stumbled across a quote from Aldous Huxley that resonated and provoked a significant step toward the light: "Experience is not what happens to a man. It is what a man does with what happens to him."

There it was in black and white. I had a choice. It really was that simple. I could move toward the light one small step at a time, or I could allow the darkness to further engulf my spirit and destroy me. I chose lightness over darkness, love over hate, and hope over despair. Ultimately, I realized that my way forward was to embrace the way Jake lived and led his life and, most importantly, to carry forward Jake's legacy of lifting up, inspiring, and serving others. It would hurt badly at times and take an emotional and mental toll on me, but I had to do it. Not just for myself, but for Jake, Liam, and Kellie.

As Jake's father, I felt a responsibility, if not a duty, to ensure that he accomplished in spirit what he intended to do while he was here with us. At his spiritual and soulful core, Jake spread joy and lifted everyone around him, from the popular to the poor, from the marginalized to the infirmly, no matter their color or creed. He brightly illuminated every room he entered as if he were a spotlight of ceaseless positivity. It was his gift, and it emerged naturally and lovingly. Example after example was unassumingly demonstrated over the course of his very brief time with us. It was the only way he knew how to exist. Now that mantle was mine to carry forward.

Days following Jake's tragic death, despite feeling unable to form a thought, sleep, or eat, we knew that we didn't need or want any more flowers. Nor would have Jake. Rather, he would have wanted to make a difference for the less fortunate and spread joy in their lives, giving them hope where none seemingly existed. So, in planning a funeral service with our church ministers at Southport Congregational Church (Jake's spiritual home), there was little doubt who Jake wanted to help the most.

In the summer of 2019, Jake participated in his first church mission trip to Pine Ridge Indian Reservation in Oglala County, South Dakota, to aid and assist the Lakota children of Red Shirt Table, among the poorest areas within the reservation. By all accounts, Jake brought delight to each day and could always be seen happily carrying children on his shoulders or reading a book to a child nestled comfortably in his lap. His loving spirit naturally drew the kids to him, and the children basked in his kindness, energy, and always-on sense of humor.

Jake returned home deeply affected by the experience, recognizing not just the incongruence but also the unfairness between his privileged background living in Fairfield County, Connecticut, and the poverty and inequalities he witnessed on the reservation. The time he spent connecting with and teaching the young children how to read and instructing them on crucial life skills left Jake yearning to help more. He was intent on bringing positive change for the Lakota children living at Red Shirt Table through his boundless energy.

We created The Jake Panus Memorial Scholarship Fund in partnership with our church specifically to ensure that Jake's desire to bring joy, aid, and assistance to the children at Red Shirt Table was fulfilled. It's what Jake was looking forward to doing in the years to come. Now he will produce consequential and lasting benefits for the children of Red Shirt Table forever.

The Jake Panus Memorial Scholarship Fund (subsequently renamed at the 2022 graduation ceremony to the Jake Panus Walk On Scholarship) provides annual post-secondary education financial assistance to children from Red Shirt Table who graduate from Red Cloud Indian School and pursue a post-secondary education. In this way, Jake's spirit will perpetually lift the children he loved and provide a tangible pathway toward their college dreams.

Two days before Christmas in 2020, Kellie and I needed to escape our house and the vapid holiday feelings that pervaded our joyless home. We walked to the beach near our home, heads down, thinking only about getting through and past the holidays. Uncharacteristically, I left my phone at home for that walk. When we returned a short while later, I checked my phone and saw a missed call and voicemail from a South Carolina telephone number. I figured it was an old classmate. Then I played the voicemail. It wasn't a call from an old friend. Rather, much to my surprise, the voice was that of the newly hired head football coach at the University of South Carolina, Shane Beamer.

Shane had been informed of our tragedy and Jake's love for the University of South Carolina and its football program by a mutual friend, Ivan Maisel. In addition to being an acclaimed college football writer, historian, and author (*I Keep Trying to Catch His Eye: A Memoir of Loss, Grief, and Love*), Ivan, who also lives in our town, had experienced his own personal trauma and grief and was all too familiar with the unwanted position I found myself in. His son, Max, sadly, passed away in 2015 at the tender age of twenty-one while away at college.

Liam and I returned the call and left our own message. An hour or so later, we found ourselves connected with Shane through a FaceTime video. Shane hadn't just called to extend condolences but instead connected in a meaningful and heartfelt manner. I was immediately struck by his authenticity and concern for Liam. The fact that he made time to call us mere weeks into his new job, when he certainly had much larger priorities at the time, spoke volumes about his character.

That conversation emerged a friendship and the genesis of an idea. I was hell-bent on ensuring that Jake realized his dream of getting to the University of South Carolina and sent Shane an email with the concept for the Jake Panus Walk On Scholarship. It would accomplish Jake's dream while fulfilling his legacy of lifting others. It didn't take long for Shane, a former walk-on football player himself, to embrace the vision I outlined. We quickly raised funds through generous friends and donors, and the endowed scholarship was born in the spring of 2021. In the process of getting to know Shane better, it became obvious that Jake and Shane shared many similar positive traits—as if they were two branches protruding from the same tree.

The scholarship provides a walk-on football player who, through hard work and perseverance, earns an athletic scholarship and contributes toward the success of the university, the Gamecock football team, and the community at large. The student-athlete will share the leadership attributes of Jake, demonstrating a motivated work ethic, fierce determination, team-first mentality, and grit on the football field. Most importantly, the scholarship will live in perpetuity at the University of South Carolina.

As Deborah Morris Coryell powerfully wrote in her book *Good Grief: Healing Through the Shadow of Loss,*

> According to the Kabbalah, the Jewish mystical tradition, a life does not truly begin until after a person dies. It's said that it is the PRESENCE that we continue to have after we are no longer PRESENT that acknowledges the power of our being. Our deeds and actions are the way we make our presence felt in the world, and to the extent that we continue to influence and impact people's lives after we are dead, we continue to live.

In this sense, Jake will forever influence and positively impact many, many children through the establishment of both scholarship funds. Dreams will become realities, and lives will be altered—this time, however, in a most luminous, positive, and loving manner. Jake's ambitions may no longer be possible, but he will, in spirit, ensure that the dreams of other children will be nurtured and fulfilled. Jake now lives on through the young men and women who earn and receive these scholarships.

A little more than one year removed from Jake's passing, I stood at a podium before a room full of college football players at the University of South Carolina, as well as the entire coaching staff and multiple cameras, and candidly addressed the fragility of life. I shared my experience as a father grieving the sudden, acute loss of his sixteen-year-old son who desired to follow in my footsteps and become a Gamecock. Beyond that, I was there with a purpose: to present the first walk-on student-athlete, Matthew Bailey, with a scholarship in honor of Jake.

Mere hours after I addressed the team and awarded Matthew the inaugural scholarship, the most vivid rainbow descended from the sky into the middle of the University of South Carolina's football stadium, Williams-Brice. There was not a drop of rain in any direction, merely a blue sky with several low-hanging cloud formations, sunshine, and the cascading spectrum of blue, yellow, and orange falling gently downward into the stadium, landing just about midfield. There was no doubt; it was Jake signaling his approval.

To say my feet were firmly planted in a realm outside my comfort zone was an understatement. Public speaking was neither something I had ever pursued nor considered a strength. I had always joked that I had a face made for the radio. Days later, my speech aired nationally across ESPN's popular *College Gameday* show, which led to more fathers reaching out to me to share and commiserate in a collective pool of grief.

Through personal tragedy, I had sourced an ability to inspire and lead—just as Jake always did. Or maybe I had discovered that it was Jake merely coming through me. Or maybe I was merely looking to "father" more kids like Jake—student-athletes who were competitive, tough, resilient, caring, and driven to make a positive impact in their communities. Whatever the reason, it felt good and meaningful. I saw Jake's joy in Matthew's face as he learned he was now on scholarship. I also had the pleasure of meeting his parents the morning of gameday. It proved emotionally taxing, and I found myself absolutely drained by game time.

I arrived at the USC versus Kentucky game that Saturday evening with two good friends from Connecticut who flew down to support me. We tailgated with old and new friends. We had been provided VIP pregame field passes and were watching the team warm up from the sidelines when I was alerted that there would be an on-the-field, pregame recognition of Jake and the scholarship. Minutes later, I found myself standing at the fifty-yard line, just about where the rainbow had descended, along with Chance Miller, senior deputy athletics director at the University of South Carolina. To my surprise, Jake and I were presented as the honorary team captains for the game. *Jake would be losing his mind*, I thought, *if he were here standing next to me on the perfectly manicured grass inside Williams-Brice Stadium.* But he wasn't. It was just me and Chance—and 80,000 rabid Gamecock fans clad in garnet and black. It's a moment that meant so much yet equally hurt, one I'll never forget.

In May of 2022, Liam and I, along with our associate minister Laura Whitmore, traveled to Pine Ridge, where, days later, we would attend Red Cloud Indian School's graduation ceremony and award two young Lakota women from Red Shirt Table with college scholarships. We were welcomed with open, loving arms by the Lakota Sioux upon arrival at Red Cloud Indian School days before the graduation. To our surprise, Liam and I were invited to participate in a ceremonial and sacred sweat lodge rite, which proved to be a powerful experience, to say the least.

The following day, on what would have been Jake's eighteenth birthday, Liam, Laura, and I hiked to the top of Black Elk Peak, the highest elevation (7,242 feet) between the Rocky Mountains in the western United States and the Pyrenees Mountains in France. Known for its vision, breathtaking views, and spiritual sacredness, Black Elk Peak provided even more to me. I wasn't just hiking this on my own. I was carrying Jake with me on each step forward. Upon reaching the peak, I gazed in every direction and had an appreciation for what author and historian Raymond J. DeMallie described in his own similar experience: "And while I stood there I saw more than I can tell and understood more than I saw."

The next morning, we returned to Red Cloud Indian School for the graduation ceremony and presented Cheree Ferguson and Ruby Good Buffalo with life-changing college scholarships. It was at this time that we decided, in conjunction with the administration at Red Cloud Indian School, that the scholarship would, similarly to the scholarship at the University of South Carolina, be known as the Jake Panus Walk On Scholarship.

The surprise and joy in the faces of Cheree and Ruby as we announced their scholarships proved well beyond fulfilling and meaningful. Jake's light, love, and joy were abundantly present in their faces. I found comfort and peace knowing that Jake couldn't have been prouder of the two young Lakota women as they prepared to embark upon their college dreams. And I was so glad that Liam was with me to experience this special moment. One year later, in May 2023, Victoria Good Buffalo (the younger sister to Ruby) was awarded a Jake Panus Walk On Scholarship, becoming the third recipient from Red Shirt Table.

Early in my own childhood, I was drawn to well-expressed positive quotations, truisms, and inspirational messages—from well-known personalities to anonymous sources. My youthful optimism fed on them like they were an energy source. The keen insights and nuggets of aged wisdom carried with them hope and motivation and reminded me of what we're all capable of achieving if we believe in ourselves, do the right thing, have a positive attitude, and never give up. I found fuel through these quotes, motivated to not only embrace them but to actually live them out and model them for my boys. They provided me with a bar, admittedly rather high, to set for living my purpose-driven life, serving to connect on a deeper level with my sons.

When Jake was old enough to read, I began a tradition of writing him daily, morning inspirational messages and positive quotes on Post-It sticky notes. The aspirational citations ranged from a variety of sources and even included my thoughts. I placed the notes directly on Jake's brown paper lunch bag or on the kitchen island where he ate his breakfast. He read them each day before he left for school. We often discussed their meaning and real-life applications of incorporating them into our daily lives, whether things were going very well or not so well. My goal was simple: to impart wisdom and inspiration into his developing heart, mind, and soul.

The custom continued with Liam. What I attempted to provide Jake and Liam was a roadmap to what truly matters in life. Through this ritual, they both understood the value of discovering their noble purposes. What I never realized was how my faith and optimism in these pithy quotations would soon be challenged on a level I had never contemplated.

The meanings I had once subscribed to fell flat in the face of traumatic grief. The words appeared hollow and empty and seemed to lack any connotation that could be applied to, let alone be accepted by, a bereaved parent. There was no space for optimism. Grief enveloped our entire house. Any perceived hope in the messages had evaporated. Unlike anything else I have ever experienced, grief freezes you in a time and place with a searing, yet inconspicuous branding, covering you in discombobulating fog.

Yet time moves on, as does life. The clock ticks forward, hours turn to days, and calendar pages are flipped to new months and years. Jake's friends and peers grow and age, changing from the sixteen-year-old kids we once knew. They return from college on their fall and summer breaks and holidays—bigger, taller, and older. They can vote. They have stories to share, and youthful energy abounds.

We, on the other hand, have an empty, quiet bedroom. The rooms and walls in our home hold photos, yet not a single new photo has been taken or added of Jake. They all stop with a sixteen-year-old boy. My mind raced, wondering how much he would have enjoyed college, yearning for the stories and enthusiastic energy that would have returned home along with him. Instead, our home barely spoke now. There was no contagious energy like before, bursting from the floorboards to the ceiling. Instead, it's sad and melancholy.

I was aware that I was amid a spiritual crisis. I searched for a way, any way, to mollify the daily agony and inspire a renewed faith in living and regaining purpose. I was bitter, exhausted, and, honestly, depressed. My life had imploded, and I was stuck in a dark place. I felt as if I lived on an island of hell, and there were days I wished to never awake again.

It was at this darkened crossroads that I awoke to the recognition that I needed to find a way to walk on through this valley of hell. I would carry this excruciating and fierce pain to my death, but moving forward and seeking to live again by honoring Jake might teach me lessons that the top of a mountain never could. I had to find meaning and purpose in the words that

I had written and, more importantly, modeled as truth to Jake and Liam. My grief compelled me to observe the connectivity between agony and optimism, despair and self-awareness, forgiveness and accountability, and beauty and suffering. The line separating each is much finer than you may think.

I missed that everyday ritual I had established with my boys. So, I started again slowly, writing messages on Liam's brown paper lunch bag he lugged to school. We never really discussed them this time. I had no idea if Liam even read a single one of them. All I did know, however, is that Liam needed me, more than ever, even if I was broken. And he needed to see and hear the unfettered truth in whatever words I shared. And if I couldn't stand for something, believe in anything, or be there for him in this calamitous moment, then what good was I as his father? We both needed to find our way to walk on from our life with Jake into the unknown—a life without him. We may not know our future, but I needed Liam to embrace what we did know: we held our future in our hands. Our pain will never go away, and the wound will never truly heal, yet I wanted Liam to know we would find a way to walk on together.

My eyes were now wide open, and my senses dynamically altered. What you see and how you envision it are wholly different experiences when you emerge from the sudden loss of your child. The previous messages and their meanings, which I had shared and lived out, only to subsequently question and discard like used tissue paper after losing Jake, resurfaced anew. The words personified a charging bull, leaving just me, the matador in the arena. Would I end up like Picasso's 1933 painting, *Death of the Toreador*? Or, instead, was I capable of rising to the challenge and uncovering new meaning where none seemed possible or plausible? As it turned out, not unlike the toreador, the closer you stand to death, the more it can motivate you to feel alive.

As I gazed at some of the quotes I had previously installed

with reverence, the words now materialized with a keener, hyperfocused significance along with a bullshit detector. It was as if the words were now placed under a microscope and magnified, provoking a panorama of elucidation on the meaning of life, dispensing with the frivolous and pointless. Getting up close and personal to death has a way of heightening your focus on what matters most, distinguishing truth from fiction and inspiration from hyperbole. It also spotlights how little you control on this planet. Spoiler alert: very little.

*Why not share this extraordinary vista of insights with others*? I thought. Didn't I owe it to Jake and Liam to clarify candor from falsehoods, most especially under the cruelest of life's circumstances?

In Native American culture, when someone passes away, they don't die, they *walk on*, meaning their journey continues. It's not an endpoint of a linear path. Rather, your journey extends into the next realm. Energy simply never dies.

At the time that both scholarships were created, I was unaware that there was an alternative Native American meaning behind the phrase "walk on." Yet there are no coincidences. The universe seemingly connected it all for us.

It's been over three years since Jake's passing, and we have awarded a total of six college scholarships in his honor, with many more to come. As Jake *walks on* and his spiritual and energetic journey continues to inspire, so does his earthly legacy of lifting up others, where it's needed more than ever. And so does my journey as his father, as I search for renewed purpose and meaning in this second act of my life.

The powerful lessons and life wisdom that emerged from my greatest loss and my journey back from the depths of darkness are designed to inspire you toward leading a meaningful and productive life—one filled with purpose and kindness and firmly rooted in resilience, courage, and service. It's what Jake would be living out if he was still here. Then it hit me. He is doing that now, just through me (and others). He was such an immense force of energy while he was physically with us that it comes as no surprise that his powerful spiritual vitality endures in another dimension, imprinting love and light from South Dakota to South Carolina and beyond.

What I hope you discover from this book is the interconnectedness of these values and attributes and how each one represents a branch on the tree of life, connected to the central trunk and deriving their energy from a common source. Just like branches, we each come in different shapes and sizes. We bend and sway and point upward and downward. Some of us snap, others fall to the ground, and we take on new purposes. Others remain whole. Yet, each of us is compelled to reveal our own versatility and confront our truths under ever-changing conditions.

We are equally connected as humans to a common source, and, like the tree of life, we each have a distinct and yet similar purpose. We are all one in the same tribe. We all suffer in some manner, and no matter what happens or how it happens, we all must *walk on* in our lives.

Jake and Liam, Summer 2020

# Motion with Meaning Leads to Living with Purpose

*"The purpose of life is . . . to be useful, to be honorable, to be compassionate, to have it make some difference that you have lived and lived well."*

—Ralph Waldo Emerson

**ABOUT SIX MONTHS** prior to Jake's birth on May 13, 2004, I approached a senior partner at the law firm in New Orleans, Louisiana, where I was a young associate attorney and made an unconventional proposal. I requested to work a four-day-a-week schedule, thereby having more time to be a dedicated father to my soon-to-be son. Foregoing a pathway to partnership was not an inquiry most senior law partners fielded. Thankfully, in my case, the request was granted.

Deep in my soul, I recognized that I valued being an involved father more than anything else, including pursuing perceived career success or the riches that naturally flowed from it. Don't get me wrong. I was still motivated to provide for my family and committed to doing my best. But I sought a balance between fatherhood and career and confidently felt I could have both. Perhaps it was my Buddha nature. I keenly understood what provided the most meaning to me and what fueled my soul. My first priority undoubtedly was and always has been my family.

And there was no more important time to be present than the early, formative years with Jake.

As I reflect upon this decision, I am eternally grateful for my choice. *Did my soul or super consciousness know something then*—that I would have such a brief time with Jake—I wondered. "You can't connect the dots looking forward," shared Steve Jobs in a graduation speech at Stanford University. "You can only connect them looking backward. So, you have to trust that the dots will somehow connect in your future." In the moment, I simply chose a pathway rife with meaning and purpose.

In light of how my life has been turned on its head, the line from that mindful decision to the crossroad where I find myself today is marked with a black Sharpie pen. It proved profound and significant. My priority in playing an indispensable role in raising Jake allowed our bond to quickly evolve and become as solid as steel. I have no regrets, as I was there for him in every way a father could dream to be. And having no regrets is crucial when someone so young and special is ripped away from you suddenly.

Together, we experienced and shared in all that life offers, from the top of the mountain down to the valleys in between. We laughed a lot and shared a ton of unforgettable, memorable life moments. While I wasn't fortunate enough to have closure or a proper goodbye by societal standards, I did say everything I ever wanted to share with Jake.

"Love you" was both a greeting and a goodbye in our home. Hugs were frequent and heartfelt. We listened to each other and were vulnerable with one another, even when it hurt. We shed tears together and shared joys. I created a list of must-see movie classics for Jake and me to watch together. When he expressed interest in possibly becoming an FBI agent in July 2020, *Silence of the Lambs* ascended to the top of the list. Sadly, it proved to be the final movie we watched together, mere weeks before he left the planet. He loved it.

I have now relived almost every memory I can recall—whether jogged by a photograph, video, personal anecdote, aroma, song, person, place, or date on a calendar—and I find peace in the fact that I taught him everything I possibly knew and shared all that I possessed. Most importantly, nothing was left unsaid between us. Jake knew how much he was loved and how proud I was of him because I told him so. And I was cognizant of how much he cherished our relationship and his family.

More often than not, we don't have to say a word in order to teach a lesson. Rather, modeling a behavior and *being it* or *living it* speaks higher volumes than *uttering it*. In this case, Jake was learning a valuable lesson merely by being an engaged and avid spectator. Showing up and being there for others matters, whether as a parent, friend, teammate, or colleague. It's one of the primary reasons we are here on the planet. It's easy to get entangled and motivated by material trappings or other temptations that draw us away from the things that truly matter in life. But it's more fulfilling to inspire, lift, or simply show up for another and be present for someone. What Jake learned early in life was simple: *humanity is about being more, not having more.*

Have you ever thought, *Why am I here on this planet?* Having a purpose behind the "why" is a universal craving we all share, no matter the language we speak or the continent we call home. Without a purpose, you're lost. We all desire to have meaning and fundamentally seek to identify it in some form with our individual existence. Mark Twain once said, "The two most important days in life are the day you are born and the day you find out why."

Sometimes the proverbial purpose light bulb is made known early in our lives. Mozart, for example, composed his first piece of published music at age five. The pathway for others in unearthing their purpose can be a long and windy one. Vera Wang didn't become a fashion designer until age forty, and Ray Kroc was in his early fifties when he purchased his first McDonald's and in his early sixties when he purchased the company outright before leading it into becoming a global fast-food brand.

No matter when your purpose is discovered, it will take hard work, dedication, sacrifice, commitment, and effort to fulfill it and live it out in a consequential manner. There is no singular road to realizing one's purpose. You must believe in yourself, push beyond fears, and conquer obstacles. You will be compelled to scale walls outside the boundaries of your comfort level. Your curiosity will be provoked and self-doubts challenged in order to understand your why.

Jake was blessed to have discovered his purpose early in life. And he instinctively knew what provided him (and, in turn, others) with the most meaning. As I look back, maybe that happened so early in his life so he could accomplish so much with what little time he would be afforded. He did more in his sixteen years than many do with a full lifetime.

No matter your circumstances in life, pursue what you're good at and fine-tune it through commitment and repetition. Your practice of your talent will become your passion. Through it all, find joy from your why. Admittedly, in the face of darkness, this may seem beyond distant, if not impossible. Trust me, I know. Finding any sense of joy after such a loss takes a lot of time. Start small. Your perspective will undoubtedly shift as you maneuver through the adventure of your life and identify your why.

Make the most of opportunities to make an impactful difference in someone else's life. When you discover your fulfillment, your meaning and purpose will be revealed.

Jake, June 2008

# Be Relentless with Your Effort as Your Attitude Determines Your Altitude

*"No one has ever drowned in sweat."*

—Lou Holtz

**IN THE MONTHS** following our cataclysmic trauma, I found myself uninspired and swimming in malaise. I was compelled to look deeper inside myself than ever before and questioned anything and everything, trusting almost nothing. Belief systems, values, and priorities were toppled by this unspeakable tragedy. What in the hell happened? Where do I go from here? Why did this happen to us? How does one recover from such a life-altering event? Who am I? When, if ever, will I feel normal again?

My disrupted mind was filled with questions. Answers were obscure, if not unattainable. I found myself indifferent, unconcerned with my lack of effort, and exhibiting a depressed attitude. I had never experienced a darkness like this. It was as if I had undergone a lobotomy. My brain acted differently, like all nerve attachments were wholly disconnected, if not severed. My memory wasn't just foggy . . . it was as if a good portion of my hard drive had been erased, and signals to my brain were undeliverable. Welcome to acute trauma, where you're not living but rather hanging on for dear life.

When this happens, the only thing left to do is to lean into your innate survival instincts. Perhaps no one has better conveyed and shared a story of survival than Viktor Frankl, the Austrian psychiatrist who chronicled his experiences and survival as a prisoner in Nazi concentration camps during World War II in the universally-revered book, *Man's Search for Meaning*.

His brilliant book was recommended by my grief therapist. In therapy session after session, I spilled my guts, revealing my innermost feelings of disillusionment, darkness, and despondency. I was lost, figuratively floating amongst a never-ending sea of dark, pounding waves, when this book landed in my mailbox.

Frankl's most enduring insight, succinctly captured by Rabbi Harold Kushner, resonated deeply the minute I read it: "Forces beyond your control can take away everything you possess except one thing, your freedom to choose how you will respond to the situation. You cannot control what happens to you in life, but you can always control what you will feel and do about what happens to you."

I was reminded of the words and messages that I had instilled in Jake. It was as if I heard it this clearly: "Dad, remember what you used to tell me? You control your effort and attitude. LFG!" Yes, I needed an ole fashioned kick in the ass, and there he was providing it for me.

I never envisioned the script being flipped on me, but that's exactly where I found myself. Liam was watching and likely wondering whether I or he or his mother would return in any recognizable, functionable manner. I'm not claiming rebounding from losing a child is easy. Far from it. Rather, it can feel insurmountable. The pain that a bereaved parent carries is unwieldy and considerable, relentless and never-ending. A broken spirit and shattered soul defy time and disregard healing as we know it, sinking you to unimaginable depths of despair.

One of the most important attributes—solely within your

control and that goes a long way toward determining success—is effort. Effort is a choice. Your choice. It does not require talent or skill. And it resides solely within you. Said another more simplified way, you get out of life what you give or put into it. Both Jake and Liam heard time and again from me that a C+ effort resulted in a C+ grade, and all that was ever asked of them was merely to give their best effort. If they did that, then we could all live with the results.

I knew that unless and until I changed my effort, my attitude would remain stuck and sullen. Effort produces joy just as much as mitochondria produce chemical energy. Was I capable of more effort, even in the face of agonizing misery, in order to get more out of life? The answer to that question was unequivocally linked to my attitude. Whether you're ready or not, you will be confronted in life with disappointments, obstacles, or, worse, life-changing adversity that will knock the crap out of you. You will be challenged mentally, spiritually, physically, and emotionally. The secret to enduring and defeating adversity and disappointment lies within you and, importantly, is solely within your control. It's your attitude.

Your outlook is one of your most valuable attributes. The ability to have an optimistic and positive frame of mind, even in the face of negativity and struggle, cannot be overstated. Thankfully, the foundation of my existence was constructed with optimism, lots of it. I owe that trait to my upbringing and parents, who I am forever grateful to for their unconditional encouragement and support no matter the circumstances. When pressed to resort to survival mode, I, fortunately, landed upon a place of familiarity—one that allowed the flickers of hope to remain partially lit during the dark, despondent state I found myself in. Instead of a crash landing on dense cement, I had the good fortune to be able to springboard from a pliant surface of promise over pessimism.

I had stressed to Jake and Liam that their effort was not only their determination and fortitude to maximize every ounce of their being but also their desire to *want* something more than everyone else. Beyond the want, it was their conviction and willingness to *sacrifice* something for it. What are you willing to give up to get what you want? Are you prepared to go above and beyond what is being asked by a parent, teacher, coach, or boss? Will you bet on yourself when no one else will? Are you inclined to invest the sweat, persistence, and dedication required to achieve your goal? Are you willing to overcome hardships and suffering, no matter the pain or cost? Can you find solutions where others concede to defeat? Can you embrace positivity while shedding negative thoughts or comments?

Whether you fully tap into your stream of effort is up to you. We all have access to the flow. Yet, only some connect the effort to the endeavor, despite the awareness that a commitment plus best effort may prove to be the difference maker. I once saw a guy wearing a T-shirt with a simple yet poignant message: "The dream is free. The hustle is sold separately." Trust me, hustle separates winners from losers and gets you noticed and, more often than not, rewarded. It's been said that hard work breeds luck. Likewise, I believe that hustle breeds hope.

In the face of adversity, you will need to unearth every ounce of your resilience. In doing so, you will experience the deepest depths of who you really are. You will bring to light your capacity to overcome suffering and, along the way, be challenged to source a level of resolve and effort you didn't even know existed within you.

Life is inherently not fair. In fact, it's far from even. Some of us are born into less-than-ideal circumstances. For others, our lives change on a dime. Wherever and however it happens, know that you are not alone in your misfortune. Nor are you flying solo in your desire to embrace an optimistic perspective in order to transform your direction. If you wish to change your circumstantial predicament, pouring positivity into a bowl of effort is the first instruction in the recipe. We all fall in life. What we land on and push off to rise back up is pivotal. Your mindfulness is your jumping-off point and the difference between surviving and thriving or surrendering and quitting.

I will never get my son back, nor will I experience the many cherished moments with him that are forever extinguished. I am left with a future filled with empty milestones, one after another, for the remainder of my life. I certainly expected to savor a long life with Jake—from college to career, dating to marriage to grandchildren, holidays, and other life moments in between. I will never, ever feel the comfort of a Jake bear hug again, his arms wrapped fully around me, his head nestled into my shoulder. That stings. A significant purpose in my life vanished, creating a void incapable of being replaced by anyone or anything.

It took time to ascend from the depths of hell. Once I released any perception of control I thought I possessed beyond my personal actions, I began to move forward again. I no longer wasted time and effort ruminating over questions or matters I simply had no control over. Negative thoughts began to dissipate into thin air.

Nothing can be accomplished without hope. The second I directed my focus forward rather than backward, a spotlight projected itself upon my effort and attitude. I began to pick up the pieces of my life and reassemble myself one hour at a time. I recognized that my effort, no matter the difficulty I faced, would kickstart the second chapter of my life. This change flipped my attitude from downtrodden to determined. It was undoubtedly a process, however, that needed to occur organically on its own timeline.

Don't waste another day of your life. Don't allow circumstances beyond your control to define you. Be the master of your effort and attitude as you navigate your life journey. Choose hope over despondency and light over gloom. Believe in yourself.

Lastly, never forget that what you feel and do in this life is up to you. The rest is bullshit you have zero control over.

# Care to Serve & Dare to Be Kind

*"Kindness in words creates confidence. Kindness in thinking creates profoundness. Kindness in giving creates love."*

—Lao-Tzu

**AS I RECOLLECT** every year of Jake's short life, there's a peace found in the wise and learned way he lived. From the get-go, he intimately understood the importance of kindness and service to others. It was obvious it wasn't even a choice, but rather the only way he knew how to maneuver on this planet. Jake truly lit up every room he entered with his joyful demeanor. What set him apart was his innate compassion and empathy for others.

Among the thousands of cards and notes we received after Jake's passing was one from a teenage girl who knew Jake from the church youth group. She wrote that she and Jake didn't run in the same circles outside of being in the church youth group and that her shyness led to her rarely attending her older sister's high school sporting events. One day, she nervously arrived at the gymnasium for her sister's volleyball game and took her seat, alone on the bleachers. Minutes later, in walked Jake, along with a few friends (Jake rarely traveled alone). He scanned the gymnasium, an ever-present smile gracing his face, and proceeded in her general direction, his friends in tow. Suddenly, he and his pals plopped down beside her, and Jake greeted her. Her anxiety melted away as Jake engaged and included her in conversation with his posse. Jake made her feel consequential and that she mattered. He knew what was needed at that exact moment and did what simply came naturally to him. In doing so, he reminds us all that each act of kindness creates a ripple, and the echoes of kindness are endless.

Service, kindness, and concern for others are held as universal moral virtues in nearly every society. All that is required is a heart. The Roman writer, Marcus Annaeus Seneca wisely wrote, "Wherever there is a human being, there is an opportunity for kindness." If ever there was a mantra to describe Jake's way of life, that may best capture it.

Jake and Liam were nurtured in the concepts of giving back to their communities and the indispensable value of being kind to others. They each instinctually and lovingly produced their own moments of philanthropy without provocation. In the weeks leading up to Liam's ninth birthday, he was asked what he wanted to do for his mid-March birthday, which fell on a Monday that year. His answer? He wanted us all to volunteer at a soup kitchen. So that's how we celebrated Liam's ninth birthday. We helped cook and prepare food, set tables, and cordially welcomed those less fortunate inside the church that cold evening for a hearty meal and a night of humanity. It was a beautiful evening shared with folks of all colors and backgrounds, circumstances, and tribulations. I watched Liam step up and embrace the opportunity to give back and connect with strangers. He discovered the depths of his compassion that memorable evening, perhaps the most valuable gift he received that ninth birthday.

Authentic acts of kindness and service mean harboring a spirit of helpfulness and empathy that connects you to others. The opportunities to exemplify kindness and serve humanity are limitless. Go ahead. Try it today. Offer someone a helping hand, hold a door for an elder, or do something unprovoked that directly aids another. Smile at someone, ask how they're doing, and listen intently to their answer. Taking the time to care or show kindness may turn a life around. Kindness is more than a behavior. It involves caring and taking an affirmative, positive step. It takes little to no effort and costs nothing to be kind and lift someone up.

The rewards are empowering. Need evidence? A recent study[1] found that children who help and serve others end up achieving and succeeding more than those who don't. They tend to thrive at school, often receiving higher grades and test results. Generous people who carry this mentality and characteristics into adulthood stand to earn higher incomes and enhanced performance reviews. Not surprisingly, they seemingly ascend the career ladder with more haste than their less generous peers. The meaning found in helping others spawns more profound, impactful, and positive relationships. Additionally, benevolence propagates creativity, productivity, wellness, and overall happiness.

The Dalai Lama reasoned, "Our prime purpose in this life is to help others. And if you can't help them, at least don't hurt them." Kindness not only dissolves the walls of misunderstanding but bestows our lives with deeper meaning. When you touch death in such a personal and jarring manner, you instantaneously deduce that the small things matter most, commencing with kindness and love toward one another.

One simple act of kindness produced the first smile I had flashed in months. It occurred in an effortless and straightforward

---

[1] Curry, O. S., Rowland, L. A., Van Lissa, C. J., Zlotowitz, S., McAlaney, J., & Whitehouse, H. (2018). Happy to help? A systemic review and meta-analysis of the effects of performing acts of kindness on the well-being of the actor. *Journal of* Experimental *Social Psychology, 76*, 320-329. https://doi.org/10.1016/j.jesp.2018.02.014

manner during one of life's more mundane moments, the kind we all often take for granted. Yet, by emotionally connecting with another, a notable mood shift occurred in me. I intuitively felt the other person's suffering on a level I may not have previously been capable of, while also witnessing the immediate benefit received by both of us. What ensued was an appreciation for our connection and shared transformation away from melancholy. Kindness affords hope to the hopeless and can sow faith in a field of doubt.

Establishing kindness and service as part of our culture doesn't happen if we only call it out one day or one week a year. Instead, the seeds for kindness and service need to be planted, watered, and nurtured. Imagine a farmer who only watered his plants one day or one month a year. Can you envision a world that rallies around kindness and service? These virtues are contagious, but only if we adopt and incorporate both into our daily lives. We don't need more random acts of kindness but rather daily *intentional* acts of kindness.

The creation of the Jake Panus Walk On Scholarship allowed me to give back through kindness at a time when hope seemed far out of reach. From the shadows and silence of grief, a purpose was manifested. It enabled me (through Jake) to lift up and help others in positive, life-changing ways, pick up where Jake left off, and accomplish what he would have wanted. This is my choice, and it's intentional and meaningful. Goodness begets goodness for the giver and receiver.

There's no disputing that I can't naturally light up a room like Jake. Frankly, not many people can. But I don't have to. The goal is to ensure that Jake's indomitable spirit, love, and light shine upon others. I have an ineradicable link with each scholarship recipient. I desire to become a part of their lives, following their progress, hearing about their challenges and successes, and counseling them along their journeys. I welcome their stories and youthful exuberance and energy. It's important to see them leveraging their opportunities while giving back to others, just as Jake has done for each of them. The baton must be continually passed for this relay to succeed. Each carries a part of Jake's heart forward in their lives, which means the world will be filled with more kindness.

What are you waiting for? Perform an intentional act of kindness today—big or small—and savor the feeling of serving humanity. Choose to smile. Be kind. Aid someone. Lift up a friend who is down. Volunteer. Make your community stronger, tighter, and more joyful. Be generous in sharing yourself with others. What we don't see is that everyone is lugging their own invisible backpack of pain and suffering. If we can acknowledge that visualization, then we can source greater compassion for one another and manifest more kindness than meanness, more service than selfishness, and more unity than division. We should strive to find connection through universal commonalities, which undoubtedly exceed any of our dissimilarities.

Elevate your kindness. Lovingly give for the benefit of others. Be the reason someone smiles, looks at you, and offers an appreciative "thank you."

Go for it: serve, care, and dare to be kind!

Jake and Carson Daly, June 2015

# Have the Courage to Be Yourself

*"Be yourself, everyone else is taken."*

—Oscar Wilde

**YOU ARE BORN** with an authentic nature and sense of self. Yet, from an early age, societal pressures prioritize fitting into someone you most likely are not, stifling authenticity from flourishing. In this day and age, when you're surrounded by the filtered, artificial, and edited social media world, it's easy to chase the wrong thing by being anything but who you really are.

Being authentic means revealing your true self to others. It takes guts and courage to fully and unabashedly embrace your authenticity and, in turn, risk not fitting in or being labeled as offbeat or different. Or worse, being rejected or shamed for standing out or speaking out. Being authentic is a primary and vital character pillar, so never trade your authenticity for anyone's approval. Most importantly, your vulnerability will reveal your courage and substance. People are drawn to genuine people, especially those who lead with their hearts and minds.

Living authentically and being true to yourself underpins your existence, identity, and reputation. Think of it as if you were born with your own authenticity chip implanted within you, not unlike a computer chip, designed specifically and only for you.

You are presented with a choice: either own it, use it, and flourish with it or disregard, override, throw on a mask, and suffer the natural consequences of not being who you really are. Herman Melville, author of *Moby-Dick*, cautioned, "It is better to fail in originality than to succeed in imitation."

If I had to describe Jake in one word, it would be *authentic*. From an early age, he possessed robust self-esteem and embraced an emotional vulnerability that defied his youth. He effortlessly related to others, listened intently by opening not just his ears but his heart, and was comfortable freely sharing and receiving thoughts and critiques. He was pure optimism, and his joy was luminous.

As his father, I stood in awe of his innately unique approach toward life. Jake was special, and everyone he encountered knew it. Don't take my word for it. Yield to the words of his friends, teammates, peers, teachers, coaches, ministers, and others who reached out after his passing:

> "Jake was one of the best friends I have ever had. He was one of the happiest kids I ever met. He wasn't like any other kid. From day one of meeting him, I instantly realized how much more confident, funny, kind, and charismatic he was than anyone else. I could always rely on Jake to just be himself and think optimistically. Jake was never fake and always spoke his mind. I looked up to Jake a lot because I could never do the things he did. Everything I was insecure about or scared to do, he could do without hesitation. Jake was one of the most unique and potential-filled kids I've ever met."
>
> "Your son was an amazing and inspiring free spirit. His smile and laugh lit up every room he entered, and his positive energy was never-ending."
>
> "Jake brought love and kindness everywhere he went

and was friends with everyone, and everyone loved him."

"Jake's exuberant approach to life was irresistible! How much we'll miss his high spirits and warm heart—and that formidable curiosity that made him seem grown up even when he was just a little kid."

"I will always remember Jake's kindness toward me."

"Jake made everyone around him a better person."

"The world is less bright without Jake."

"Jake always made everyone smile wherever he went."

"Who knew that such a precocious, exotic, fun little boy would become such a joyous, well-rounded, and beloved inspiration?"

"Jake exhibited and played with so much joy both on and off the field and treated every person who he met with such friendly and warm love."

"Life without Jake will not be easy, but I know he would want his beliefs, his life, and his enthusiasm to live on each day."

"Jake was a stunning individual, in looks, attitude, and composure."

"As your coach, I had the pleasure of watching your smile inspire and contagiously spread to all those around you."

"Jake was one of the only people that helped drag me out of a deep hole I was in."

"I remember thinking how empathetic Jake was as a fifth grader."

"Jake brought an intensity to any game he played because he challenged others to rise to the occasion and be their best."

"Whenever we encountered Jake, he carried with him an omnipresent energy . . . and his spirit and vitality seemed to have no boundaries."

"Jake understood how to relate to anyone."

"Jake was an ambassador of God's love."

"Jake stood out with that amazing thick blond hair and contagious smile."

"He simply was the brightest, boldest light ever."

"Jake would look at you like no one else. . . . We were all taken by Jake's charisma and charm."

"Jake was exceptional, a shining star, a one-in-a-million kid."

"He always knew how to comfort anyone when they were feeling down."

"Jake was always someone I looked up to for his thoughtfulness and confidence."

"I feel sorry for the planet now that Jake is gone."

He was unabashedly comfortable with who he was. He understood that being authentic was a recognition of who you fundamentally are and a willingness to proudly and boldly be that person. He was larger than life, brighter than any star in the sky. A true ambassador of joy and fun. Little did I know, he was a professor emeritus teaching us a master class on authenticity.

The genesis of authenticity emanates from your heart more so than your mind. Yet choosing to be your authentic self is a compilation of your values, beliefs, and choices repeated often and over time. Ultimately, being true to yourself becomes a habit so ingrained in your daily existence that it directly benefits your emotional and mental well-being.

Your confidence and courage to express uniqueness will serve you well in overcoming pressure to cede to conformity or the wishes of others. Trust me, it will not always be easy to maintain your authenticity, as you will be pushed, pulled, or even cajoled to be someone else in order to fit in or feel included. Don't surrender. Instead, stand firm and honor and celebrate who you are and the principles and values that form the bedrock of your purity.

The conundrum for any bereaved parent is that there is nothing authentic about the dreadful grief experience. On the contrary, the level of shock, pain, and overwhelming spectrum of emotions that instantly befall you when abruptly informed that your child is dead are foreign and unfamiliar. You no longer feel like yourself, thereby making it impracticable, if not impossible, to be yourself. Your life as you knew it ended that fateful day. Everything is blown to smithereens. The challenge and fear become not just whether you will ever feel right again but also whether you will be able to have faith in being your true self ever again.

It took time (lots of it), but I eventually was able to accept that while my grief certainly may have felt inauthentic, my ability to survive such a loss and source meaning and purpose amid the darkness couldn't have been any more authentic. The veracity of who I was at the core, thankfully, never wavered or changed. My brain grasped the concept that I inhabited a world where everything was impermanent, but my heart could never have prepared for the reality that Jake would be removed from this Earth in a nanosecond.

I was overwhelmed and smothered by a chain reaction of trauma. Despite enduring that, I thankfully remained unapologetically original in attending to my sorrow. I openly tear up and cry out of the blue, including in public, as emotional triggers arise from routine to uncommon occurrences. I am candid and blunt in describing the anguish that I now bear and the fresh life perspective I now offer. I openly and unapologetically share Jake's stories and say his name aloud, indifferent to whether that makes anyone uncomfortable. What I came to honor is that if any healing was going to occur, it wasn't about returning to my old life. Rather, the quest was to remain my authentic self in this new, unplanned trajectory of life I was dealt.

When you embrace that which makes you come alive with

vitality, you discover your most precious commodity: who you really are. Jake reminds us all that we are born with one obligation, to be authentically who we are.

# Character Is Just as Important as Talent

*"Integrity is doing the right thing, even when no one is watching."*

—C.S. Lewis

**IT WAS ESTABLISHED** at a very young age for Jake and Liam that I cared about who they were, what they stood for, and that they lived with integrity. These attributes were nonnegotiable. They were encouraged to think critically, ask questions, and do the right thing based on an instilled family value structure. They undoubtedly understood that their principles, beliefs, and actions defined their being. By doing so, others would know what they stood for and represented, leaving no doubt as to their moral fiber.

Being a person of integrity is wholly unrelated to any title or position you hold. It's about the way you conduct yourself in your daily life. Whether you are building a friendship, business, marriage, community, team, or culture, integrity is a necessary foundational pillar. Without a strong footing established with integrity, you will undoubtedly fail.

People with integrity tend to be trustworthy, reliable, admirable, and confident. In fact, the best leaders possess integrity, which, in turn, allows them to inspire others to follow and trust them. They tend to receive greater buy-in when they speak, as well as when they share their vision. Possessing talent may receive praise and adulation, however, it lacks staying power and eventually fades away. Whereas talent is perceived as a gift, integrity is a superpower that transcends every facet of your existence. Peter Schutz, the former CEO of Porsche, wisely counseled, "Hire character. Train skill."

Living with integrity breeds respect and meaningful relationships. Your integrity will be tested again and again in the ordinary course of daily life, and your choices, words, and actions will honestly reveal your ethics. Exhibit the courage to stand up to peer pressure or opposition, most especially when it compels you to walk what, at the time, may feel like a lonely road. Trust me, if you have integrity, you won't be lonely for long or, likely, at all. Conversely, you will be welcomed into circles of opportunity for adding value to the lives of others.

Do you lead your life by not compromising who you are for the sake of personal gain, approval, or fitting in with others? Can people take you at your word? Are you capable of maintaining promises and owning up to your mistakes, even in the face of being unpopular? Are you the same person on and off camera or in the spotlight as well as in the shadows? Are you open to accepting criticism?

Acute grief is a disruptive force, unflinching in its intensity. It undeniably produces doubt where certainty once existed and seeds skepticism in your values and beliefs. In this sense, it posed a direct threat. Who I was in this state of grief felt entirely different. I needed to resuscitate my belief system. This jarring and disruptive experience had uprooted part of my foundation. I was in moral distress and challenged to meet my integrity in an alley of darkness, where I no longer felt strong, brave, or wise. When you lose a child, you take it personally. I asked myself over and over, *Why did we let him go on the trip?* And when you blame yourself and are swimming in a sea of unpredictability, it can feel as if nothing truly matters anymore. In many regards, the only conclusion you seemingly accept is that whoever you were and whatever you formerly thought failed you. I was unrecognizable to myself, which can be terrifying.

I was encouraged to have faith that I would one day be whole—but certainly a much different person. I recognized I would be rebuilt from the inside out. Yet, in my darkest moments, there was always a flash of hope infiltrating my ruptured existence, from which emerged a rekindling of faith in myself. My still-beating heart would be entirely reconstructed stitch by stitch. Thankfully, it would embody the same moral fiber that previously wove it. I may have been broken, but I lived with a heightened capacity for empathy, compassion, and love. The new life force that began to pulsate through me was unmistakably noble in every regard.

When we received Jake's phone back from the Rhode Island State Police, it took me days before I had the mettle to unlock it and peek inside. When I finally did one Saturday morning, what was revealed, unsurprisingly, was a final, shining example of Jake's defining character.

His telephone log showed an incoming telephone call thirty-five minutes prior to the crash, followed by Jake returning the call to the same 203-area-code phone number nineteen minutes before the crash occurred—his last phone call ever. Curious who called him and who Jake called back for his final cellular outreach, I decided to dial the number. I grabbed my phone and started punching the numbers into my cell phone, oblivious that it was 4:30 in the morning, when, suddenly, my phone recognized the number among my contacts, and a name popped up on my screen. It was Marlene Sheehan, our eighty-year-old neighbor whom Jake adored and admired and often assisted with her gardening, weeding, moving of furniture, snow shoveling, dump runs, and a variety of other assorted chores. A former schoolteacher, Marlene had graciously tutored Jake in literature one school year. She loved and cared for Jake as much as anyone and treated him like a son. Jake loved helping her and had profound respect for her strong sense of self and unadulterated manner of living life to the fullest. She challenged Jake intellectually, and he returned the favor by amusing her endlessly. Tired of weeding her vast and colorful gardens one summer day, a young Jake looked up at her, sweat pouring off his brow and running down his face, and exclaimed, "When I get my own house one day, the entire front yard will be concrete!" She howled at his youthful and exuberant perspective.

I listened to the voicemail Marlene left for Jake that August Sunday morning. She was unaware Jake was away for the weekend but wondered if he could possibly help her in the coming week with a project in her yard. Jake dutifully returned that phone call mere minutes before he left the planet.

There is no substitute for your character. It's a difference maker and game changer. And if you build it and nurture it correctly, your integrity will stand the test of time.

You must stand for something in this life. But if you lack integrity, I'm not sure you can stand for anything.

The first two recipients of the Jake Panus Walk On Scholarship at the University of South Carolina: Payton Mangrum (85), Me, and Matthew Bailey (34)

# The Magnitude of Gratitude

*"When you arise in the morning, give thanks for the food and for the joy of living. If you see no reason for giving thanks, the fault lies only in yourself."*

—Tecumseh

IT WAS 3:30 a.m. on a balmy, dark July morning in 2019. In a barely lit church parking lot with other parents, we awaited the youth group's return from their mission trip to Pine Ridge.

Jake stepped off the bus wearing his hat backward, like he often did, and with his thousand-dollar smile lighting up the early morning blackness. We hugged. Nobody gave better hugs than him; he enveloped people with love, so much so that they affectionately became known as Jake bear hugs. As we clung to each other, he said, "It was amazing, Dad. The children are incredible. But . . . they need our help."

Upon arriving home, Jake bounded up the stairs, eager to wake his mom and share his experience despite the early morning hour. He was fully awake, and soon, so was his mother. He hopped onto our bed, sunk in next to his mom, and began scrolling through his cell phone, sharing picture after picture of the young Lakota children he aided with reading and other life skills. He regaled us with stories of the games they played as well as personal anecdotes about each one of them. He rattled off their names, described their personalities and less-than-ideal homelife situations, and advised of their challenges and fundamental needs. The depth of the connection Jake made and the impact it had on him was transparent.

He concluded by solemnly noting the stark differences, unfairness, and inequalities between growing up in Fairfield, CT, versus Pine Ridge, SD. Jake was impacted in a visceral and profound way. He openly shared how his perspective was broadened and how his blessings were taken for granted at times. What emerged from his experience was a deep desire to make a positive impact and meaningful difference in the lives of the young Lakota children. He spoke of them like brothers and sisters, his expression of love obvious and unmistakable.

Jake couldn't wait to return to South Dakota the following year. He was determined to be an influential change agent, shining a ray of hope in their lives. The power of gratitude was not lost on him. He could distinguish between needs and wants, recognizing the connection between his gratefulness and the ensuing joy. Sadly, the June 2020 mission trip was canceled due to COVID-19. Jake was beyond disappointed—deprived of the opportunity to return to Pine Ridge.

Have you ever noticed that it is near impossible to be thankful and unhappy at the same time? Not dissimilar from effort and attitude, whether you have gratitude is a transformative and powerful choice. Your choice. Being grateful steers you away from despair, redirecting you from a negative sinkhole toward the positive influences and blessings that surround you.

Gratitude is a positive emotion reflected in self-awareness that transcends individuality and connects you to greater humanity. It goes beyond saying "thank you" and instead demands appreciation for your existence and blessings, from the mundane to the material, the microscopic to the copious. It's a recognition for those who support, aid, and inspire you along the way.

Health benefits are derived from expressing and finding gratitude in your life, as difficult and challenging as that may be at times. Psychologist Robert Emmons, one of the world's leading scientific experts on gratitude, defines it as "an emotion, a virtue, a moral sentiment, a motive, a coping response, a skill, and an attitude. It is all of these and more." Indeed, gratitude comes in an array of shapes and sizes and fits countless life contexts. It can be a character trait, altruistic disposition, and superpower state that connects your past, present, and future. This likely led Cicero to the conclusion that gratitude is "the mother of all remaining virtues."

How do you start your mornings? Do you take time to quietly reflect and acknowledge your blessings, whether few or many? Or do you simply take things for granted and live in autopilot unappreciation? Are you more focused on what you don't have than what you do? Do you find yourself craving more? Do you give thanks prior to eating dinner, honoring your good fortune, however small or large? Author and philanthropist Germany Kent eloquently shared this keen perspective that illustrates the positive impact of embracing gratitude: "It's a funny thing about life, once you begin to take note of the things you are grateful for, you begin to lose sight of the things that you lack."

I have found that making time to mindfully keep a gratitude list is incredibly beneficial. Try it. Commit to writing down one original thing you are grateful for each day for thirty consecutive days and check in with yourself and your list after one month. Are you happier? Are you living more in the present moment? Are you more capable of seeing the good versus being bogged down by the negative? Do you appreciate what you have versus what you lack? Did it lead you to connect to others and strengthen relationships? Singer, songwriter, and activist Willie Nelson admitted, "When I started counting my blessings, my whole life turned around."

When you lose a child and your family lineage is broken in unrepairable fashion, any sense of gratitude is promptly stamped out. Rather, you feel violated and assaulted. The thought of being grateful is ostensibly incomprehensible. On the outside, gratitude and grief appear to be polar opposites. Yet, with time, I was enlightened to learn of their interconnectedness. As it turns out, gratitude and grief are united in a unique and relevant manner. Gratitude is a pivotal quality that not only sustains you but can save you. It lifts you up when you think you can't stand. It's the rescue boat when you are sinking in a sea of despair.

In the weeks following Jake's death, I recall being told that I was lucky to have had Jake in my life, even only for such a short time. My initial reaction was less than positive. Grateful? How am I supposed to be grateful for having Jake *for only* sixteen years? I felt shortchanged, was rightfully pissed off, and certainly believed I didn't need to lose my son in exchange for a lesson on gratitude.

But then one day, admittedly two years into my grief, I found myself lying prone on the grass, fully stretched out, staring into a sunny, cloud-free blue sky when a thought emerged: *what if Jake had never been in my life?* That was the moment that gratitude gripped me and shook my soul awake. My mind flashed through a series of happier and more joyful memories with Jake. One after another. A smile graced my face. If all life was ever going to give me was sixteen fleeting years with Jake, then I was indeed a lucky man. Don't get me wrong; losing him still hurts, and it always will. I know that will never change. Yet I have found comfort and gratitude that he was in my life, and I thank God he made Jake part of my plan.

You must find a reason to be thankful in your life, no matter your circumstances. Acknowledge the love, support, and help from others. Reciprocate it. Don't wait to be struck by trauma, disaster, or loss to realize the difference between the paramount and the trivial. Having gratitude won't just turn your life around;

it will guide you toward the meaningful and magical. It will connect you with humanity, fostering more joy for you and others, which is something the world sure needs.

Don't waste another day. Cultivate your gratitude!

Jake and Liam, Ipswich, MA July 2020

# Accountability: Your Choices = Your Consequences

*"Accountability breeds response-ability."*

—Stephen R. Covey

**TAKING OWNERSHIP OF** your words, behaviors, and actions is a fundamental building block that paves the road toward advancement and prosperity. When you assume ownership in your life, you are liberated from engaging in blame and shame and will look to problem-solve rather than attack others when things don't go as planned. Trust me—things will definitely not go as planned. Roadblocks will appear out of nowhere. Obstacles will be placed in your way. Problems and dilemmas will arise, and mistakes will certainly be made.

Ever-quotable Hall of Fame football coach Lou Holtz reminded his players of the value of accountability: "The man who complains about the way the ball bounces is likely to be the one who dropped it." Holding yourself—and others—accountable not only inspires confidence but builds trust. Louis Nizer, the loquacious, successful trial lawyer to the famous, once forewarned, "When a man points a finger at someone else, he should remember that four of his fingers are pointing at himself." Holding yourself accountable enhances your ability to correct and learn from mistakes, allowing you to take control of decisions and, ultimately, your life.

Accountability is an indispensable trait that makes you reliable, responsible, and trustworthy. In fact, it's a defining characteristic of true leadership. The late, legendary women's basketball coach Pat Summitt preached, "Responsibility equals accountability equals ownership. And a sense of ownership is the most powerful weapon a team or organization can have." If you aspire to be a leader, whether as a student, parent, coach, or CEO, then creating a culture of accountability begins with you and your actions. What you model for others is what you will eventually build. When you model and act with accountability, you provide undeniable proof for others to believe and trust in you.

There are no days off. Leaders are measured by many things, but among the first items on that list is accountability. Without it, you are bound to fail. If your friends, classmates, teammates, or colleagues can't trust or rely on you to do the right thing at the right time, then why should they be interested in following your lead? Joe Dumars, who won NBA championships as both a player and executive, submits this enlightened takeaway: "On good teams, coaches hold players accountable; on great teams, players hold players accountable."

Teaching children how to be accountable goes far beyond a parent commanding an order or instruction and expecting it to be followed to the letter. Rather, accountability is achieved by allowing space and time for the child to make their own choices, unmotivated by any potential incentive or punishment. Being accountable means you have the discipline and ability to discern the right choices on your own and do the right things in your life.

Jake and Liam heard time and again that their choices ultimately shaped them and, importantly, that those choices equaled their consequences. They equally learned from their good choices as much as from their bad ones. Taking ownership of your words and deeds is a compulsory step in personal growth and development. During your life, you will make numerous decisions and carry out ensuing actions, many small and daily and others more monumental in nature, which involve calculated risks. No matter what, the choice of how you respond to whatever and wherever you find yourself in life is yours. Satirist P.J. O'Rourke summed it up this way: "There is only one basic human right, the right to do as you damn well please. And with it comes the only basic human duty, the duty to take the consequences."

No parent desires to see their child fail or fall short of a goal, yet the only way our youth will ultimately learn to assume responsibility for their words, behaviors, and actions is to provide them a runway to either lift off or stay grounded by fear. You can't do it for them. Your job as a parent is to prepare them for these moments, which they will meet whether you like it or not. Would you rather have your child meet the moment head-on and be prepared? Or is your preference to misguidedly coddle and insulate your child from the realities and harshness of life?

All teenagers seek freedom from their parents, exploring the boundaries and limits. Jake was no exception. Yet, when he made a mistake or disobeyed a directive by his own choosing, he quickly accepted and owned the natural consequences of his choices and actions. In the early summer of 2020, I asked Jake to return some library books, situated across from our home, a short walk away. At the time, Jake was mere days from securing his driver's permit and anxious to get behind the wheel. I looked at our driveway a few minutes later and noticed our truck was missing. I promptly walked to the library.

As I came around the corner and approached the front door, my eyes locked on Jake, exiting the truck he parked neatly into a parking space. He looked up, surprised to see me. With his head tilted downward, he sheepishly smiled as he approached me. I calmly asked him, "What in the hell are you thinking, driving the truck here?" He responded like a teenager. "Dad, it was just across the street, and I thought I'd get some practice in." At that moment,

I didn't find his answer as funny as I do now. I grabbed the keys, returned the truck safely across the street, and waited for him to emerge out of the library, cross the street, and return home. We sat outside in our yard, and I explained the array of potential consequences and liability that could possibly have ensued from his choice. The responsibility that came with operating a vehicle was made abundantly clear, and he accepted the discipline that resulted from his boneheaded decision. It was a teachable moment, yet one that also came with consequences. Days later, Jake aced the exam and proudly secured his driver's permit.

To be accountable to others, it is incumbent that you first master being self-accountable. It is axiomatic that poor decisions lead to negative consequences. How do you avoid making bad choices? For starters, pause and think it through before you act (a tall ask for teenagers). Query people you trust to gain a fresh, and often objective, perspective on the matter. Trust your intuition and always avoid taking the easy route. Often, the right choice is the more challenging or difficult pathway. In fact, the right thing and the hardest thing are likely the same thing. No matter what, you will inevitably make a poor choice along the way. Don't get discouraged. It happens to everyone. Apply your lessons and learnings moving forward, as there will always be another choice to make and an opportunity to redeem yourself and mature.

Accountability—like effort, attitude, and integrity—comes from within. Are you detecting a pattern by now? Your capacity for your inner strength to prevail over your outward fate resides within you. You have to struggle sometimes and other times quietly reflect in order to source your own way out. Additionally, your attitude will play a vital role in your decision-making. Is it positive or negative, bitter or better, open-minded or constrained? While it may be your choice, the consequences typically extend far beyond yourself. "Choices made, whether bad or good, follow you forever and affect everyone in their path one way or another," penned author J.E.B. Spredemann.

Taking accountability for my overpowering grief allowed me to view it, and myself, in a fresh, new light through a lens of deep introspection. I realized how much I needed to reduce my own expectations, not only of myself but of others. I needed to set healthy new parameters and practice self-care to protect my broken heart. Previous prescribed societal expectations flew out the window. We benefited from having a renowned and wise Boston-based grief therapist, Mitch Davidowitz, as an ally and friend in our foxhole. We were thankfully introduced to Mitch by a mutual friend from Boston during our frantic search for a therapist following the loss of Jake. We met over Zoom in early September 2020 and immediately bonded, connecting as if Mitch were an old friend. Initially, we met three times a week as Kellie and I were shells of ourselves and felt like we were walking a high wire in bare feet—completely unstable and erratic, in total shock, and gutted to the core of our soul. We were absolutely lost and despondent, existing as if we were zombies, and unrecognizable in many regards. Mitch was not just a game changer; he was a lifesaver. To this day, we still see Mitch, and he continues to serve as a vital sounding board to my darkest thoughts and fears, providing inspiration to flashes of insightful growth. Despite being my therapist, I consider Mitch a dear friend, even somewhat of a father figure.

Over the last forty years, Mitch has trained healthcare and mental health professionals around the United States in the compassionate care of those facing loss and aided bereaved parents around the world with bearing the unbearable. In addition to his extensive clinical background, Mitch has trained intensively in mindfulness practice since 1974, studying extensively with Ram Dass and Stephen Levine. Mitch was born to do this work; he's masterful in his thinking and listening, sage-like with his words, and has a heart filled with love and compassion. He is an internationally coveted grief therapist. I realize now how fortunate we were to have crossed paths with Mitch, and I am beyond grateful that he had availability in his beyond-busy schedule at our darkest hour. We may not have survived without Mitch on our side.

For starters, Mitch helped me understand that I needed to be accountable for my grief to ensure my initial bitterness and rage didn't leak out and cause harm to others. Time was a critical factor in aiding that process. I found healthy, productive ways to honor and process my grief and diffuse my anger without punishing others in false and unintended ways. Mitch coined the phrase "vigilant mercy" and implored that both Kellie and I practice and embrace it, not only with each other but equally with others. "Vigilant mercy" became a phrase heard often in our home.

Most people run from grief as if their pants are on fire (for obvious reasons). It's hard, painful, and gutting to be with an acutely bereaved individual or a couple. It's boggy ground to walk. The unsteadiness and wide array of life changes make your life feel disjointed and irregular. I accepted that old friendships faded while new ones sprung up like tulip buds in early spring. I didn't take it personally because, prior to August 9, 2020, I was as ill-equipped for the task as anyone. I was clueless about how to properly comfort someone in grief. I, too, lacked the right words and didn't understand what was needed. Nor was I comfortable sitting with someone immersed in extreme suffering and unforgettable anguish.

Admittedly, it is hard to be present with someone in visible (and invisible) grief for any extended period. It's dark territory. But grief is as much a part of our lives as the air we breathe. It's universal. And death is indiscriminate. We are all affected by it. We just attempt to convince ourselves otherwise . . . until it happens.

At some point in the process, responsibility for what remains and what you can do about it surfaces. You yearn to feel alive again as you maneuver back and forth between despair and hope. Kellie and I held ourselves accountable to each other and acknowledged the effect of our words, mood, and behaviors toward each other and others. We chose to be intentionally gentle with one another, viewing each other as damaged souls, bent over and puking into a toilet. That visual image of one another enabled us to stave off unnecessary misunderstandings, avoid turning our anger against one another, and elevate the compassion and empathy we needed for each other to survive this horrific, life-changing event.

I learned to accept help and support in ways I had previously shunned. We established clear boundaries of what we were comfortable doing and not doing and implemented a practice of self-care as a fundamental priority. I learned how to provide aid, lend an ear, sit in silence, and speak without opening my mouth. Our needs and wants came first. It had to be this way.

I recognized that mistakes happen in grief, too, just like in life. And that is okay as long as you are accountable. Life is a laboratory for trial and error, and with that comes the propensity for missteps and mistakes. Equally, it provides freedom to redeem and correct them. Don't associate shame or any negative connotation with making a mistake. Instead, normalize and learn from it. The imperfection presents a new opportunity and encourages resilience and additional effort, rather than giving up.

Ever hear the phrase, "Shit happens?" Well, it does, and with much greater frequency than you'd like to admit. It is not just okay to make mistakes, but it's necessary to learn and evolve. Basketball coach Rick Pitino offers, "Failure is good. It's fertilizer. Everything I've learned about coaching, I've learned from making mistakes."

Mistakes happen every day, big and small. If you acknowledge that, then you appreciate that it is unhealthy to exist in a state of worry or fear over committing one. A fearful, worried person sees an obstacle, whereas a fearless, resilient person attacks the problem head-on. Humorist Erma Bombeck captured the stagnation that worry offers: "Worry is like a rocking chair: it gives you something to do but never gets you anywhere."

Note your missteps and be open and willing to grasp the lessons that naturally flow from them. You learn by doing, and by failing, you're able to discover your next steps and move forward. Legendary UCLA basketball coach John Wooden stressed the importance of learning from mistakes with this line: "If you're not making mistakes, then you're not doing anything."

Own your mistakes, just as much as your victories. In doing so, you will reveal who you are and what you represent. Framing it another way, I encourage you to make positive shit happen from your mistakes. Ultimately, every challenge in your life, every problem, and every option comes to make you or break you. The choice is yours—whether you become a victim or the victor or accept responsibility and hold yourself accountable.

Own your choices and accept the consequences that flow from them. Every morning you awake to a choice: remain asleep with your dreams or arise and fearlessly and responsibly chase them. Choose wisely!

Jake, August 2, 2020, one week before he died

# Realize Your Resolve & Discover Your Genuineness

*"For me, every hour is grace.*
*And I feel gratitude in my heart each time*
*I can meet someone and look at his or her smile."*

—Elie Wiesel

**WE HUDDLED WITH** family and dear friends under a tent on a rainy Sunday morning on August 16, 2020, to lay to rest the ashes of Jake in the memorial garden outside of our church. Our friend and minister, Paul Whitmore, shared the notable words of French philosopher, Pierre Teilhard de Chardin: "We are all spiritual beings on a human journey." When you regard life in this light, you access an awareness of your connectivity to one another. Likewise, it compels a focus on our impermanence on this planet.

What affects you certainly impacts others. And vice versa. To endure and evolve in this life, you must find your grit and reveal your grace. You can't succeed with one and not the other. Both are necessary and enduringly linked.

On a late September Saturday morning in 2021, I stood among a throng of people congregating on the campus of the University of South Carolina's historic grounds known as the Horseshoe. I brought Jake to these hallowed grounds several times, and returning without him felt more than odd. This

U-shaped plot of land, listed on the National Register of Historic Places, was hosting the *SEC Nation* pregame show. I was invited on the show for a live interview with Marty Smith to discuss the scholarship, which was awarded just days prior.

Marty and I were cordoned off and surrounded by a crowd of Gamecock enthusiasts as a video portion of my speech to the team aired on multiple screens. When the video ended, they cut to us. "First of all, I just want to say on behalf of everyone here, your grace is astounding," offered Marty. I can honestly say that I lacked any awareness of my grace at that moment. I was there for Jake, plain and simple, and Marty's words didn't even register in real-time. This was live television, and I was focused on whatever question he was about to ask me so I could provide a coherent answer and not stumble, mumble, or cry. There was little doubt that Jake was there with me, holding me upright and infusing me with the steel necessary for the moment.

While waiting to board my flight home the next morning, I was shown a video of the interview by a friend. With the benefit of reflection, I texted Marty, *I believe it's more grit than grace that allows me to be still standing.* With added contemplation over the next week, I concluded, however, that it didn't matter whether there was more grit than grace or the other way around. Both are essential attributes that shape your character and serve you in your journey.

Where, how, why, and when you encounter your grit and grace may range from the mundane to the memorable. In my experience, it organically happened, and the timing and magnitude proved cosmic. Grief strips you down to nothing and eventually exposes grit and grace, or your lack thereof.

It's easy to spot in another because it's so recognizable by your soul. While my suffering is undoubtedly different from yours, the gift of healing available to each of us is universally similar and relatable, no matter the injury, adversity, or setback. You just need a little grit and a lot of grace to get through the experience.

Your grit may determine whether your life journey defines or defeats you. It's your inner fortitude and mental perseverance to stand up to the winds of agony. It's your capacity to prevail under trying circumstances, to see the light amid the darkness. It is the password that opens the door leading you away from the abyss. Grit isn't bestowed upon anyone. It must be earned.

"Grit is living life like it's a marathon, not a sprint," advised psychologist and author Angela Duckworth. Your raw endurance and steadfast refusal to let go of a dream or goal is honed every day you awaken and simply say, "Yes, I can." You must believe in yourself and your determination to conquer any challenge.

Grace, on the other hand, is the emotional intelligence bestowed upon you by God. Or, as Pope Francis described it, "It is the amount of light in your soul." That light resides in all of us and must be internally kindled in order to shine and be realized. It's your capacity to exhibit kindness, compassion, empathy, and love toward yourself and others, even when it's seemingly complicated and arduous. In the end, do unto others as if you were the others.

Grace can be difficult to explain but obvious when you observe it. It stands up and boldly shouts out. It's evident, remarkable, and palpable. Singer/songwriter Jeff Buckley eloquently described grace as "what matters in anything—especially life, especially growth, tragedy, pain, love, death. That's a quality that I admire very greatly. It keeps you from reaching out for the gun too quickly. It keeps you from destroying things too foolishly. It sort of keeps you alive."

Jake's grace was striking and noteworthy. His prodigious presence as a mere toddler left many adults speechless. Jake was self-aware on a level many never achieve. He instinctively knew who needed to feel connected and loved, who could use a hug or a laugh, who required to be heard or validated, or who needed a smile to brighten their day.

One card we received following Jake's passing perfectly encapsulated Jake's grace. In the summer of 2017, our entire family participated in a community grassroots bike ride that supported cancer survivor programs. Jake and Liam's papa (Kellie's father) was battling cancer, so this family activity took on special significance. After riding twenty-five miles, Jake, thirteen at the time, joined us as we attended a post-race party at the home of friends in our neighborhood. What happened next is vintage Jake.

"Jake was an exceptional, shining star. I knew he was a one-in-a-million kid way back when we were first lucky enough to get to know the Panus family," wrote a family friend in her note to us. "We were at the post-bike event party when the host's niece with special needs was getting lost in the commotion of set-up, people arriving, food, beverages, what have you. Jake intuitively knew that she needed some TLC. So, while no one was watching, and without his parents' prompting, Jake initiated a wonderful, warm, engaging conversation. He had her smiling and laughing, and a friendship was formed. I watched with amazement from a distance—it made a strong impression upon me. I formed my own little friendship with Jake, and I loved (and will cherish) every encounter I had with him. Jake was so outgoing, personable, funny, compassionate, intelligent, and loveable. Jake will never be forgotten."

The luminosity of Jake had no boundaries in his physical life, nor can it be contained now in his spirit life. What I knew then of his grace has only been magnified in his passing. Exactly twenty-two days after Jake died, August 31, 2020, I was inside our house when I received a short and direct text from Kellie. *Come outside and look up.* Kellie was outside making telephone calls in search of grief therapists. I darted out our mudroom door and spilled out onto the driveway, where I found Kellie lying down on a pea stone walkway, cell phone to her ear, looking skyward and pointing up. I spun around and looked upward. The light was so blinding that I had to immediately don my sunglasses to view it.

I had never seen anything like it before. Above our house hovered the most immense circle of light surrounding the sun. It reminded me of a scene from *Close Encounters of the Third Kind* and appeared as if an alien ship was parked directly over our home. I stared in disbelief and awe. In Native American lore, these sightings are called Whirling Rainbows or Sun Dogs and can be interpreted as a sign of looming change. Other religions, including the Kabbalah, suggest it is God's presence or spiritual energy powerfully coming from above, purporting to offer relief at a time of great need. What is observed is a full circle of light around the sun, sometimes rimmed by a circular edge of a rainbow, which is a result of the sunlight's bending by high, lean, icy clouds. This natural phenomenon lingered over our home for well past one hour.

Since then, we have been blessed to catch sight of four additional Sun Dogs: one in November 2021, another in December 2022, a fourth on June 21, 2023, and the fifth on August 9, 2023—the three-year marker of Jake's passing—while away on a family coastal getaway in New England. The second Sun Dog occurred while Kellie and I were spending a weekend getaway at a friend's remote home nestled at the end of a dirt road in bucolic East Hampton. After a beautiful, serene weekend tucked away from civilization and hidden in a home that overlooked the Acabonac Harbor meeting the Napeague Bay, we were packing up and carrying our bags to the car when, out of nowhere, appeared a sun halo on a Sunday morning. Again, it hung high above us, as if meant for us.

One year and one month later, while flying from Connecticut to South Florida to visit family over the holidays, Liam looked out the airplane window at 35,000 feet and espied our third Sun Dog. This time, the silhouetted image of our airplane was reflected within the middle of the circle of light.

On June 21, 2023, I was working from home when I received

a phone call from Lindsay Czarniak, a friend and sports media personality with Fox Sports. Lindsay was on her way from her home in Connecticut to the airport when she telephoned me to discuss travel plans for a trip to Saratoga Springs, NY, later that summer. Suddenly, she exclaimed, "Oh, my God, Stephen. What was that thing called that you told me about before? Where you saw a rainbow around the sun?" Before I could respond, she continued, "I am seeing it now. And it just came out of nowhere when I called you."

I ran outside to find Kellie relaxing on our back deck and looked skyward. There it was again, the fourth Sun Dog, again situated high above our home. Lindsay had never seen one before. Now she understood. For us, it was yet another welcoming sign from Jake, and it arrived on a day when Kellie felt the void of Jake not being with us more than ever and yearned for her beloved child. A recurrence of four in your life is said to suggest a need for persistence and endurance, qualities certainly necessary to prevail in overcoming adversity, most especially the loss of a child.

We've come to believe that this is one way, among many, in which Jake communicates with us. So, it was only fitting that on the third-year marker of his passing, we found ourselves sitting outside on a brilliantly sunny afternoon on Cape Ann, Massachusetts, solemnly honoring the time of his passing, when Kellie suddenly pointed skyward and yelled, "Stephen, look up." And there it was, the fifth Sun Dog we had seen in three years, hovering over and enveloping us like a warm blanket. Again, prior to losing Jake, we had *never* seen such a sighting. Never.

If grace truly is the amount of light in our souls, then Jake continues to be a beacon of light, enabling those blessed to see and feel it to navigate their lives with heartfelt love and grace for one another.

Find your inner light and allow it to illuminate the world. Be generous with your grace and gallant with your grit!

# Change Is the Only Constant

*"Change is inevitable. Growth is optional"*

—John Maxwell

**IT'S ACCEPTED THAT** death is an all-embracing part of our human experience. But it still leaves you feeling shattered and dispirited in unimaginable ways, most notably when it is someone you adore and love dearly and when it happens suddenly and without warning. "The death of a beloved is an amputation," shared writer C.S. Lewis, who lost his mother when he was a small boy, only to later lose his beloved wife to cancer shortly after their marriage.

Life does not stop for anybody or anything, including grief, which comes in many forms. Your son, daughter, mother, father, or grandparent may have passed on. Your job may have been eliminated. You may find your marriage irretrievably irreconcilable. A life-threatening diagnosis may have been revealed. Your home may have been destroyed by a hurricane or wildfire. Still, the daily tasks and conventional regimen continue. The twenty-four-hour news cycle spins forward with never-ending stories of more tragedy than inspiration. The seasons of sport march on. Leaves flutter off their branches, the holidays come and go, and winter turns to spring, followed by summer. Babies are born, and people die. Roman emperor and stoic philosopher Marcus Aurelius offered, "Loss is nothing else but change, and change is nature's delight."

While initially grieving, you are counseled against making any major life changes for at least a year, even though you desire to run far, far away. I presume this is suggested with the thought that any significant change may compound your grief with additional problems. Or it may prove to be more than you can handle. There is little doubt that you have scant capacity for anything other than your grief. Ironically, everything around you continues to change—except you. Your life after losing a child is completely mutated into an unwelcome shape you simply don't recognize. You may consider relocating and changing houses, but moving only changes the view. There simply is no escaping what you are contending with and who you are now. Better said, no matter where you are, there it is. Grief follows you everywhere.

Society further encourages you to let go of your loved one in order to move forward in your life. I flatly disagree with this notion on its face. Rather, for any healing to occur, you must eventually let go of the suffering, not the loved one. You are pressed to confront this challenging and, at times, complex, conundrum head-on and with whatever remnants of your heart remain. People will attempt to tell you they know how you feel. Yet it's deeply personal and overwhelming, individualized on a scale no one else can truly understand. It's unrelatable to all except those who have endured the pain. You question the purpose of pain. Eventually, I accepted that part of Jake's soul inhabits mine, and a fragment (or more) of mine departed with him. He is eternally my son as I carry grief and love onward, shedding one while amassing more of the other. Helen Keller said it best: "What we have once enjoyed deeply we can never lose. All that we love deeply becomes a part of us."

If you accept that change is constant, then you honor that the place you find yourself in is temporary. Your reality is ephemeral.

Despite this recognition, you often treat time, change, and your station in life where you find yourself, whether good or bad, as more fixed or permanent, as if your feet are stuck in concrete. Without change, there would never be a past or a future. Everything in life unfolds as a moment or phase, and there is a beginning and an ending to each. If you watch a leaf float down a stream long enough, it will eventually fall out of eyesight. The stream, like life, will bring forward new leaves. So, don't get too comfortable. Life is a constant curveball, and more pitches are on the way. Change will occur whether you welcome it or not.

There is little doubt that change breeds stress, tension, and disruption, sometimes even chaos, especially since most change is out of your control. Your power to choose your response to change is all you superintend, making the choice rather simple: embrace it or resist it. There's a Cherokee proverb that provocatively inspires moving forward from change: "Don't let yesterday use up too much of today." By flexing your mental reservoir of strength, you are better positioned for personal growth and pliancy in the face of uncertainty. You must be mindful to not allow uneasiness or worry to foster inaction. On the contrary, when you conquer your apprehension to change, you take ownership, minimizing any pessimism that may arise while opening yourself to new experiences and opportunities.

Change is not only coming; it's happening around you now. Be open to it and allow your resilience to guide you through whatever change comes your way, from slow curveballs to heat-sinking fastballs. As Charles Darwin astutely noted, "It is not the strongest or the most intelligent who will survive but those who can best manage change."

Embrace change!

# Most People Never Run Far Enough/Your Determination Will Define You

*"It's hard to defeat a person who never gives up."*

—Babe Ruth

ON MARCH 4, 1993, legendary North Carolina State basketball coach Jimmy Valvano took the stage at the ESPY Awards, announced the creation of the V Foundation for Cancer Research, and delivered an unforgettable message: "Don't give up. Don't ever give up." His words still ring loudly and reverberate today, inspiring many and carrying great weight and wisdom no matter the cause, malady, or obstacle one is facing.

Giving up is a choice, and it's easy to quit. And once you do it, you are more likely to do it again and again. It takes determination, fortitude, and a never-say-die attitude of unbending resilience to outweigh the forces of concession. Former New Orleans Saint and ALS survivor and advocate Steve Gleason coined the slogan *No White Flags* to capture the spirit of not only refusing to give up but gaining strength in the face of challenge. It has since evolved into a symbol of the human spirit—perseverance in the face of insurmountable obstacles. No matter your affliction, suffering, or struggle, embodying the spirit of Gleason's mantra will benefit you.

There is arguably nothing that knocks you down harder than

losing a child suddenly and at such a young age. The intensity of the trauma that ensues makes giving up an enviable option for many. For parents and siblings, it's natural, as scary as it sounds, to be overcome with desirous feelings of not wanting to live under these unwanted circumstances. I know one set of parents who lost a child who discussed whether one parent should join their dead son while the other parent stays behind with their living children. Rational thoughts don't necessarily surface at the top of a grieving brain. Instead, you find yourself swimming in a pool of hell with seemingly no exit that offers compelling consolation. Personally, it was a struggle within my family, and it required colossal strength, limitless love, and loads of therapy to work past those dark thoughts.

Thankfully, giving up was never part of my DNA. I had just lost one son, and there was no goddamn way I was going to lose anyone else. I was compelled to exercise every particle of resilience within me. That foundational characteristic proved invaluable for me and my family. In this case, however, the stakes were much higher. The context was staggeringly different. The conditions were more elevated and strenuous than anything I had ever encountered.

In the context of a "civilian life" (a phrase Ivan Maisel introduced when describing the fortunate souls who never lost a child), I preached to my boys the significance of building a strong resilience muscle. A similar lesson was instilled by my parents. Time and again, my father and mother always encouraged me, in the pursuit of a dream and, most especially, during a setback. "Get knocked down, get back up" was a refrain that still rings in my ears and I came to champion during trying times. I am forever grateful for having that potent message implanted into my soul.

Reality check: we all fail, suffer a setback or loss, or fall short of a goal or desire. During life, it will occur multiple times. But don't be fooled. Failure is merely a step closer to success for those determined enough to continue forward. "Many of life's failures are people who did not realize how close they were to success when they gave up," imparted inventor Thomas A. Edison. Whether you know it or not, you can rise up, press on, and learn from your failures. You just need to demonstrate a relentless determination to never give up. The Japanese offer a proverb that captures this spirit of resilience: "Fall seven times, stand up eight."

Easier said than done? Not really.

Do you have a goal or dream? Are you willing to commit to achieving it? Does an inner hunger drive you to thrive, no matter what is placed in your way? Have you been dealt lemons in life? It's universally recognized that one of the key attributes of success and achievement is the will or tenacity to endure. "With ordinary talent and extraordinary perseverance, all things are attainable," proclaimed Sir Thomas Foxwell Buxton. A more simplistic pronouncement was made by Scottish hymn writer and minister George Matheson: "We conquer by continuing."

Were you aware that in the early 1990s, a young, unknown rapper was rejected by every record label he pursued? Undeterred, he created his own record label and released his debut album. Nearly thirty years later, Jay Z has released thirteen solo studio albums, four collaboration albums, one live album, one compilation album, and one soundtrack album. He was the first hip-hop artist to become a billionaire. What if Jay Z had thrown in the towel when no one but himself believed in him?

Did you know that Walt Disney was fired early in his career for not having good ideas? Then his first animation company went bankrupt. But he never quit. Instead, he persisted and ultimately went on to build the iconic and multibillion-dollar Walt Disney Company.

Stephen Spielberg was rejected by the University of Southern California's School of Cinematic Arts not once but three times. His response? He simply went on to become a celebrated film director, producer, and screenwriter, winning three Academy Awards.

Actress Emily Blunt's childhood was challenging. She grew up with an incapacitating stutter. She tried working with speech coaches, but it didn't help. Yet she didn't give up. Nor did her coach, who suggested she try acting classes instead. As it turned out, that was just what was needed for her to overcome her speech impediment. Today, she is a world-famous actress.

A young woman was raised in poverty by a single teenage mother. She was molested at nine, became pregnant, and lost a child at fourteen. One of those events alone is enough to defeat people. Not Oprah Winfrey. She forged ahead with resilience and tenacity and overcame adversity. She believed in herself while others doubted. Her drive and confidence served as inspirational fuel in the chase for her dreams. By nineteen, she was a coanchor on the local evening news. Ultimately, she became one of the most successful, influential, and philanthropic personalities on the planet.

In 1972, Joe Biden suffered a personal tragedy just one month after winning the US senate election in Delaware at just twenty-nine years old. His wife, Neilia, and their one-year-old daughter, Naomi, were killed in an automobile accident. An unspeakable, tragic catastrophe. He found a way to move forward, carrying both intense grief and aspirations to make a difference. He went on to lead a long, successful career as a public servant that culminated in becoming the president of the United States in 2020.

Rob Mendez was born with no arms or legs. He moves with the assistance of a custom-made, motorized wheelchair that he operates with his back and shoulders. Despite the overwhelming odds, he became a successful high school football coach in Southern California, author of the book *Who Says I Can't*, and an ESPY Award winner of the Jimmy V Perseverance Award. Rob is a shining example of the mind's power to conquer challenging circumstances.

Michael Jordan, arguably the greatest basketball player ever, was cut from his high school team his sophomore year. That singular event energized Michael and led him to the University of North Carolina, where he scored the game-winning jump shot in the national title game in 1982. Subsequently, he was drafted by the Chicago Bulls in 1984 with the third overall selection and, over a fifteen-year career, became a six-time NBA champion, six-time NBA Finals MVP, five-time NBA MVP, and fourteen-time NBA all-star.

No matter what happens or where you are in your life, keep going and never stop trying! There are countless stories just like these where individuals overcame immense odds or turned rejections into unbridled successes. Having a tenacious outlook requires you to be fearless toward failure, resilient over rigid, and adaptable above inflexible. Amelia Earhart, a daring thrill seeker ahead of her time and the first female aviator to fly solo across the Atlantic Ocean, owed much of her success to her tenacity. "The most difficult thing is the decision to act. The rest is merely tenacity. The fears are paper tigers. You can do anything you decide to do."

Importantly, tenacity is a learned skill, deriving its roots from life participation. You can't be a spectator and expect to be rewarded. You need to jump in and partake in all that life offers. Inventor Charles F. Kettering offered this timeless nugget of wisdom: "Keep on going, and the chances are that you will stumble on something, perhaps when you are least expecting it. I never heard of anyone ever stumbling on something sitting down."

Celebrated self-help author Napoleon Hill proclaimed, "Effort only fully releases its reward after a person refuses to quit." The next time you get knocked down, passed over, dealt a bad hand in life, or turned away, remember that your fortitude to never, ever quit will determine your fate. Film and fashion icon Audrey Hepburn shrewdly emphasized that "Nothing is impossible. The word itself says 'I'm possible'!"

Make this your mantra: I persevere. I am relentless. I keep going. I walk on.

Everything and anything are possible . . . just as long as you don't ever stop believing and running toward it!

Rock stars: Post Malone & Jake, 2018

# The Little Things Are the Big Things

*"The little details are vital.
Little things make big things happen."*

—John Wooden

ONE OF THE vital differences between success and failure is related to one's attention to detail. It takes lots of little things performed well and with passion for big things to occur. By doing the little things correctly, you will add value to your pursuit and others'.

Doing the little things is simultaneously simple and powerful. Yet many search for shortcuts or compromises in their quest to arrive at the bigger thing. Sadly, society places an accelerated and much brighter light on attaining big and bigger things. Consequently, many lose focus on the far-reaching implications of their small, daily decisions and purposeful steps. Don't let it be lost on you how much each little step restores hope while connecting you deeply to the smallest things in your daily life. More importantly, "If you can't do the little things right, you will never do the big things right," sensibly cautioned Admiral William H. McRaven. While doing the little things precisely doesn't always bring instant acknowledgment or validation, skipping them most assuredly will frustrate, if not derail, your pathway toward achievement and happiness. Basketball legend Michael Jordan insightfully pointed out, "Step by step. I can't think of any other way of accomplishing anything."

No matter your goal or vision, will you have the patience to put in the necessary work, one step at a time? Are you committed to doing the little things right, no matter how many steps it takes to achieve success? Will you arrive early and stay late after practice to master a weakness? Will you put in the time and effort when no one is watching? Are you prepared to do the menial tasks in your job without complaint in order to advance in your career? Renowned artist Vincent Van Gogh recognized, "Great things are not done by impulse, but by a series of small things brought together." Rarely is there a fast track to your desired dream. That's why Lao-Tzu's wisdom stands the test of time: "The journey of a thousand miles begins with one step." Without each modest step, one methodically after another, you will never reach the pinnacle. Have you ever seen anyone climb a mountain in one step? I haven't.

What is most often perceived as insignificant in the moment may, with the passage of time, take on a level of heightened significance. It's not what you ultimately arrive at but rather what you did to get there and who supported you that will produce the most treasured memories. Rarely will you do it alone. The journey usually involves the encouragement and support of others for you to reach the big things and fulfill your dreams. Don't ever lose appreciation for the time and effort someone else contributed to lift you up or inspire you toward your goal. Whether it was a teacher or coach, parent or boss, mentor or minister, someone invested themselves and their time in you. Each particular and painstakingly meager step mattered. Actress Liz Valley shrewdly opined, "Notice the small things. The rewards are inversely proportional."

Similarly, it takes very small steps to climb out from under the cloud of grief. Initially, the focus is centered around self-care. For starters, the mere act of getting out of bed proved more challenging than you'd think. From there, I confronted the prospect of changing out of pajamas into clothes. The next logical step led me to shave, shower, and care about my hygiene and appearance at a time when I cared very little about much. The loss of appetite elevated the need for frequent, daily hydration reminders. I lost fifteen pounds in weeks.

Months into my grief, the process evolved into finding a reason to leave our house for walks in nature. I desperately sought a change of scenery and ever-so-brief flashes of respite. Awakening to see an early morning sunrise, walking barefoot across a sandy beach, and hearing the melodic song of a bird perched high above on a tree branch proved to be the tonic of nature my soul beckoned. Immersing myself in nature reminded me of the scale of the universe and the connectivity to the circle of life by which we are all bound. A dead flower of winter is soon replaced by a blooming bud pushing upward through the soil of spring. "Little things console us because little things afflict us," cleverly advised French mathematician and philosopher Blaise Pascal, who lost his mother at the age of three and, sadly, later his wife.

For bereaved parents, the little things mean everything. This is due to the fact that our brain capacity has shrunk to the size of a grain of sand, and our perspective has done a complete volte-face. It's understandable that many are afraid of saying or doing the wrong thing around grievers. Choosing the right words is no easy task, even for the most compassionate. However, ignoring the pain and sorrow of a bereaved parent only serves to compound their grief.

Everyone grieves differently, so accept them as you find them. This is their grief, not yours. There is no fixing or solving it for them, so release that notion now. You must accept that you cannot alleviate or assuage their pain. It's perfectly okay not to have a single answer or words for whatever happened. What you can do, however, is show up. Sit with them and validate their unbearable grief by being present in their darkest hours. You can be honest and vulnerable. You can hug them, cry with them, and hold them tightly without having to open your mouth. If you want to say anything, say how sorry you are, and stop there. Understand that being there for them without ever uttering a word is all that is required. This is about their pain and not yours. Don't run away or avoid them because of your inability to cope with awkward and uncomfortable emotions triggered by grief. The significance of showing up for them when their life appears to have no meaning is more consequential than you may ever know.

Intense loss upsets the normal routine of life in every conceivable way. So, if you want to know what you can do to help a family member or friend in grief, here's a few ideas. Rather than attempting to make their pain go away (you won't), make their day easier by proactively bringing them a meal. Walk their dog. Mow their lawn. Run an errand for them. Do anything that lightens their day-to-day responsibilities. Do their grocery shopping. Just do anything that helps them get from one day to the next. Most importantly, do it without asking if they want it done.

Don't tell them that God needed another angel to justify the loss of their child. Don't tell them how lucky they are to have other children. Don't tell them that time heals all wounds. Don't suggest that they will eventually feel better. Don't attempt to tell them you understand how they feel. Or that their child is in a better place now. Those messages ring hollow and fall flat, producing additional pain where it's certainly not welcomed or needed.

Instead, just be present, love, and support them. Be unafraid to honor their loss or say their child's name. Don't shy away from sharing a story or favorite memory about their child. Offer them photographs you have of their child. These actions are deeply meaningful and represent more than just a little thing to bereaved parents, who cherish every photographic memory of their child, especially ones they don't have or may have never seen before.

Six months after losing Jake and with the country still mired in a COVID-19 shutdown, we fled the icy, cold February winter of Connecticut for the warmth and serenity of remote North Captiva Island, a barrier island rising from the Gulf of Mexico, off the southwestern coast of Florida. One afternoon, we set off on a walk down the unspoiled, secluded beach with friends who were visiting us. We found ourselves alone on the beach, which stretched the western side of the island. A short while into our meandering stroll, I had to peel off from the group for a cell phone therapy session. I slipped into the dunes for privacy and to shield myself from the strong gusts of wind. I settled into a sunken pit of sand nestled between the tropical hammock vegetation and the shoreline. Kellie, Liam, and our friends continued slowly onward.

Nearly an hour later, I emerged from the dunes back onto the beach. I spotted them encamped about 150 yards away on the white sand. As I approached, Kellie, who had been a nonbeliever in signs, waved me over. She said, "You're never going to believe this. I was walking and thinking about Jake when I said 'okay, Jake, you want to give me a sign? Then go ahead and give me a sign. But it can't be some seashell or even a seahorse. No, it has to be something more substantial.' Seconds later, this washed ashore at my feet!" She spun around and pointed at the shoreline. I looked over her shoulder; my jaw dropped. Before my eyes was an immense, dead sea turtle.

Cultures around the world acknowledge that a dead turtle represents the death of one way of life and the beginning of another. The sea turtle is a symbol of endurance and vigor, indispensable traits for weathering any transition, and an indication of loss and coming transformation. In Native American culture, the turtle embodies a connection to Mother Earth. The turtle's shell is often seen as a metaphor for the sky, and the creature is known to be able to travel between the physical and spirit world.

Over 1,100 miles away, on a trip to escape the horrors of home, merely wandering a deserted, little beach, Jake made our souls smile. In the hustle and bustle of today's fast-paced, ever-changing, busy world, smiles may be taken for granted. Never underestimate the power of a smile. Taking things for granted diminishes joy. One small expression of love, in this case, reflected our eternal inseparability with Jake. Author Nikki Rowe expressively wrote about the connectivity of our souls when she penned, "Our souls speak a language that is beyond human understanding. A connection so rare the universe won't let us part."

What you manifest in life's big moments is manufactured through the small ones. The little things provide hope when the big thing feel distant and, perhaps, unachievable. They can also lift you up when you're sorrowful and inspire you when you feel empty.

The summertime weeks leading up to Jake's date of passing always present an emotional challenge for me. My anxiety rises, as does the pain, moving upward from my gut to lodging in my throat. As the three-year marker quickly approached, I found my body tightening, my heart yearning for my son, and my head pounding with apprehension of the upcoming reliving of the horror. There's no way around it. August 9th will always be a day of renewed dark agony, as if a monster is awoken inside me with the singular goal of endlessly haunting my soul.

Then I received an unexpected and out-of-the-blue email. It was a small gesture that brought with it a wave of hope and light at a time when I needed to grasp a buoy to stop myself from sinking and being overtaken by the thunderous waves of grief. Among the first talks I delivered after my speech in South Carolina was a motivational speech to the Staples High School (Westport, CT) boy's lacrosse team in the early spring of 2022, prior to the start of their season. A family friend introduced me to the coach, Will Koshansky, suggesting I talk to his team. Will is an accomplished lacrosse player, having starred for the University of Pennsylvania and later playing professionally in Major League Lacrosse for the Chesapeake Bayhawks and Rochester Rattlers. He was entering his third season as the head coach of the Staples lacrosse team and was intently building a program designed to do things they had never done before. The expectations for that upcoming season were high, and he welcomed me with open arms.

I shared my story and the enduring legacy of Jake with the boys, some of whom knew Jake and many who had played against him at Westport, the next town over, bordering Fairfield, CT.

I stared into a roomful of determined, youthful, and energetic teenage eyes, sensing their eagerness to kick off their season, filled with such promise. I encouraged them to play as a team, love one another, lift each other up, and practice and play with one heartbeat and one goal: to win the state championship, something Staples lacrosse had never done, competing at the highest, most competitive level in a state known for its high-level lacrosse. I attended several games and tracked their progress all season, which culminated with them defeating their rival and number-one seed Darien in the state championship in a masterpiece performance, 12-3. They finished the year ranked number one in Connecticut, number eleven in the country, and the number one public high school in the country by *Inside Lacrosse*.

But they were far from finished. Despite losing a large class of seniors from the 2022 team, they repeated as state champions in 2023. I wrote Will a simple, belated congratulatory email, praising him for the achievement and lauding him for his effort and determination in building such a successful winning culture at Staples. Here's the reply I received from Will weeks later as I approached the year-three marker of losing my son:

> *Stephen—*
>
> *I appreciate the message. I will be honest—this year, right before playoffs, we lost to Ridgefield in an ugly, sloppy, terrible performance. The loss meant we wouldn't have the best record in the FCIAC and receive the #1 seed for playoffs—something Staples has never done. We've been #2 a couple times in my handful of years. But never #1. We let that slip away with an awful game, and I was devastated. So angry and frustrated and sad and pissed afterward.*
>
> *About an hour or so after the game, I was still pissed and opened up my phone to Twitter. The very*

*first tweet I saw was by you. I don't remember exactly what it said, I think information about one of the ways you were raising funds for the scholarships—but immediately, I thought about Jake. And the immense loss your family went through, and how angry and frustrated and sad and devastated your family must have felt. And I realized how selfish I was being, feeling sorry for myself like I had been cheated out of something I deserved when there were so many amazing things I needed to be grateful and feel lucky for. Genuinely, that night changed not only the trajectory of this season but of my own growth as a coach. It was an inflection point for me, where the rest of the way, I tried really hard to catch myself and remove any thoughts and desires to win for my own benefit and instead win for the kids I am coaching.*

*I spoke about this moment and the way I tried to act afterward at our end-of-season banquet. I basically summed it up as I felt like, before that moment, I coached from a place of anger—angry that I felt like I didn't get the recognition I deserved, that I needed to prove people wrong, that I could make Staples the best—to coaching from a place of love—where all I tried to focus on was the relationships with my players and having success for their benefit.*

*I believe it will prove to be a pivotal moment in my coaching career. And it all started with Jake. His impact is still happening in ways you couldn't even imagine. Thanks.*

*—Will*

Savor the little things in your life. They matter the most.

# Power of Hope/
# No Mud on the Brain

*"Hope is faith holding out its hand in the dark."*

—George Iles

**IT'S BEEN SAID** that hope is the conviction that your future can be better than your present and past. Well, when your child dies, so does hope. It is sucked out of you in one fell swoop. At that moment, it feels like the world has come to a screeching halt. Everything stops, except the clock, calendar, and life. Yet, a bereaved parent can hardly move or feel anything, the least of which is anything positive. The only future a griever sees is one filled with emptiness and darkness.

With the emptiness comes negativity. What did we do to deserve this? That's right—when you lose a child, it feels personal and decidedly unfair. Your traumatized mind seeks to chase down every theory and angle. You crave to understand. Yet answers are nowhere. They simply don't exist.

Hope is (or at least should be) a basic part of every human life. Air. Water. Food. Shelter. Sleep. Hope. I had always possessed hope, a lot of it, in fact. Finding myself nearly hopeless, even if only briefly, was depressing. Everything felt insurmountable. My thoughts stirred amid irrationality. Author Madeline L'Engle deftly posited, "Maybe you have to know the darkness before you can appreciate the light." I wish that wasn't true, but like many things in life, you often take much for granted until it's no longer available to you. Or worse, taken from you. My new world was seemingly moonless. Aristotle said, "It is during our darkest moments that we must focus to see the light." I was compelled to concede to my circumstances and blindly seek that which was invisible.

Hope is not linked to your expectations, desires, any certainty, or particular outcome. Rather, hope is your fuel-injected power source that fosters an innate belief within you. It propels you forward, most especially during challenging and difficult times. As Dr. Judith Rich wrote, "Hope is a match in a dark tunnel, a moment of light, just enough to reveal the path ahead and ultimately the way out." For me, that moment of light occurred when I rekindled the recognition that my new journey wasn't reliant upon external forces. Rather, it existed within me. Day after day, I deliberately crawled toward the glint of light and leaned into my faith to source a scintilla of hope. William Sloane passionately wrote, "Hope arouses, as nothing else can arouse, a passion for the possible."

Negative energy is also something we are all compelled to confront, experience, and hopefully defeat in our lives. How often have you received a negative, baseless, or unwanted comment and, yet, taken it to heart or allowed it to rattle around inside your head? Are you surrounded by people who gravitate toward negativity and, in turn, suck your positivity or hope like a vampire drawing blood? You must repel negative thought. Mahatma Gandhi proclaimed, "I will not let anyone walk through my mind with their dirty feet."

Your ability to construct and master a positive attitude and clutch hope over misery will aid you in deflecting and avoiding energy suckers. You must develop a Teflon shield that prevents negativity from demoralizing and sticking to you. Misery loves company, and negative people gravitate toward a pit of despair and darkness. Their preference is not to be alone in this slide downward.

In the weeks following Jake's passing, I experienced an array of well-intentioned interactions offering condolences. Some of the expressions landed like a lead bomb. I accepted that grief is foreign for so many, and few can speak its language. The best explanation, perhaps, is this: You don't know what you don't know. How could someone who hasn't experienced such a catastrophe even begin to understand? In my broken heart, I knew they meant well. I opted to find off-ramps to quickly disengage from any negative or uncomfortable conversations. It didn't serve me to carry negativity forward or hold onto rage. When I am asked, "How did your son die?" My reply is, "No, let me tell you how he lived."

As you evaluate your own life and ponder those who you surround yourself with, the question is simple: who do you want in your foxhole with you? People who tell you what you can't do? Or those who inspire and provoke the best out of you? You decide. Businessman and philanthropist W. Clement Stone once said, "There is little difference in people, but that little difference makes a big difference. The little difference is attitude. The big difference is whether it is positive or negative."

Negative people don't solve problems; they create them. They rarely overcome adversity but instead are defeated by it. Sean Stephenson was born with osteogenesis imperfecta, stood three feet tall, and was relegated to a wheelchair. Despite the adverse circumstances, he became a renowned motivational speaker. Allow his sage insight to inspire you: "If someone tells you, 'You can't' they really mean, 'I can't'."

The journey begins from inside, where hope resides. It is a very powerful element of your existence. Jonas Salk, who discovered the polio vaccine, stated that "hope lies in dreams, in imagination, and in the courage of those who dare to make dreams into reality." Without hope, your life may seem dreadful, your future bleak, and your potential may appear as nothing more than a permanent state of despair. By the same token, you may succumb to defeat with haste, become paralyzed by anxiety, surrender your sense of faith, or become destitute of any vision of positive possibilities.

Martin Luther King, Jr. prudently sermonized, "We must accept finite disappointment, but never lose infinite hope." Being able to cradle hope helps you envision a pathway toward positive options. You will be inspired to chase hopeful avenues filled with optimism. And you will likely attract like-minded support from others along the way.

The late Buddhist monk, Tich Nhat Hanh, urged that "hope is important because it can make the present moment less difficult to bear. If we believe that tomorrow will be better, we can bear hardship today." When you hope, you recognize that things are always evolving, believing that a better hour or day awaits you.

Choose hope over despondency. Courage over fearfulness. Light over darkness. Inspiration over disenchantment. Don't allow your soul to surrender. Holocaust survivor and Nobel laureate Elie Wiesel encouraged that "hope is like peace. It is not a gift from God. It is a gift only we can give one another."

What are you waiting for? It's your time to foster hope.

Never forget, the quality of your mindset ultimately architects the quality of your life.

# Don't Fumble Your Honesty & Humility

*"Pride makes us artificial and humility makes us real."*

—Thomas Merton

THE MEASURE OF your interpersonal relationships thrives or dies with your honesty and humility. As a musical legend and pioneer in country music's Outlaw movement, Waylon Jennings bluntly expressed, "Honesty is something you can't wear out." It's a revered, respected character trait. Thomas Jefferson observed that it's "the first chapter in the book of wisdom."

Honesty transcends lying or deceit. It is your moral compass, guiding you to think truthfully, speak honestly, and live with sincerity. If you are unable to say what you mean and do as you say, then most of your relationships will topple like a house of cards. Humorist Josh Billings summarized honesty as "the rarest wealth anyone can possess." Without honesty, you won't be considered as someone who can be trusted or relied upon. Being honest also encourages others to reciprocate with frankness, opening up vulnerabilities and leading to genuine connections. The Beatles legend John Lennon noted the importance of honesty in friendships when he quipped, "Being honest may not get you many friends, but it will always get you the right ones."

Humility, that feeling that you have no special importance

that makes you better than any other person, brings to light your genuineness toward others. Do you stop and say hello to the janitor in your school, the doorman in your apartment building, or the security guard in your office building? Do you view others as equal regardless of what they do, where they are from, what they earn, or where they live? Gordon B. Hinckley, the former leader of The Church of Jesus Christ of Latter-day Saints, intelligently recognized, "Being humble means recognizing that we are not on earth to see how important we can become, but to see how much difference we can make in the lives of others." I dare you: make a memorable difference in the life of another.

A collection of research studies concluded that humble leaders listen more effectively and, in turn, embolden better teamwork, resulting in greater success than leaders who demonstrate less humility. Do you respect a difference of opinion? Do you care what others think and believe? Do you encourage open dialogue and free-flowing ideation? Are you someone who inspires collaboration and a team-first mentality?

With humility, you are also able to self-identify your weaknesses and mistakes. French Renaissance philosopher Michel de Montaigne wrote, "On the highest throne in the world, we still sit only on our own bottom." Jake understood his strengths and weaknesses. But he positively lived his life focused on the consequential virtues that directly benefited others.

Jake's instinctual desire to produce a laugh had no boundaries and often showcased his humility. He loved a good joke or funny prank. We learned of two stories after his passing that particularly epitomize his humility and humor. Both occurred with his church youth group peers during their 2019 mission trip.

The first came to us via an unsigned note. It read,

> *Dear Panus family,*
> *I am so sorry for your loss. I would like you to know*

*that Jake always brought laughter to people's lives. Last year during the mission trip, I remember that we went into a Target to get some supplies for the camp. Jake, always one to bring happiness to those around him, went into the changing room and came out wearing a dress. Needless to say, we were all laughing so hard it hurt. Even some random people nearby were chuckling. That is how I will remember Jake: someone who was always trying to brighten people's lives.*

The second story was told by a lacrosse teammate and classmate of Jake's, Kieran Heske, during the annual youth group-led service at our church five months after Jake's passing. He commenced by explaining a long-standing mission trip tradition to the congregation. At the conclusion of the mission work, an ice cream social had been held for decades. Part of the ritual required the boys to ask the girls to the ice cream social. Jake, a rising sophomore, shared with Kieran and some other pals that he intended to ask a girl named Hannah, who was four years older. She was regarded as one of the prettiest and nicest girls. Kieran recalled thinking that was pretty brave of Jake.

A few days before the fast-approaching social, most of the kids were gathered outside their living quarters playing games. Unbeknownst to everyone, Jake climbed onto the roof of the building, looked down at his peers, and began serenading Hannah with the theme song from *Hannah Montana*. Heads quickly turned and looked up in disbelief and awe as Jake performed his a cappella rendition. He concluded by asking Hannah to go with him to the social in front of everyone. To the surprise of no one, she said yes.

Classic Jake—bold, confident, genuine, and honest. His absolute fearlessness was on full display in that vulnerable, public moment. He radiated humility through his actions. Those fortunate enough to cross Jake's path knew they were heard, seen, and, most importantly, loved.

Cultivate your own honesty and humility, for they will serve you well in your journey.

Jake, age six

# Outside Perspective Leads to Inner Reflection

*"Some people see the glass half full. Others see it half empty. I see a glass that's twice as big as it needs to be."*

— George Carlin

**YOU ARE INFLUENCED** by your perspective, which is constrained by your experiences. If your existence to date has resulted in more disappointment than joy, then you may be limited in how you approach and view things. But if you can expand and widen your perspective, then you may change your circumstances and the way you observe life.

Oscar Wilde proposed, "The optimist sees the donut; the pessimist sees the hole." Have you ever been encouraged to step into someone else's shoes to gain a greater appreciation for their predicament? Learning to take the time to respectfully listen to how others experience life is the first step. Being open to hearing the differences in accumulated knowledge creates an enduring capacity for tolerance. Further, it results in a more evolved approach toward conflict resolution and avoiding potential misunderstandings. If you can listen intently, you will gain an appreciation that other viewpoints exist beyond your own. "And those who were seen dancing, were thought to be crazy, by those who could not hear the music," declared Friedrich Nietzsche.

One of the learnings from my grief is how instantaneous my outlook on life was dramatically altered and reshaped. It was as if an on-off switch was flipped when my ears heard and my brain processed the news. The old me no longer existed. *Poof!* Who was I now? The version of myself I had known for fifty-one years was gone, never to be truly accessed again. In many respects, it was as if my memory and brain were scrubbed clean, erasing an entire history of feelings, beliefs, and more. Born anew from the shock and trauma was a soul bewildered by tragedy, one whose senses were shaken and stirred, if not transformed, to such a degree that I didn't recognize myself, and I certainly didn't feel like myself. I found myself in a wholly unrelatable reality, where I lost interest in just about everything.

In one casual get-together with our minister, I revealed experiencing a sensation as if I was sitting on the edge of the globe, my feet dangling into the abyss of darkness, finding myself as close to touching the next realm as I had ever been. Not only did I sense a connection to the spirit world, but I felt, heard, and saw things from the other dimension in numerous ways and varied settings since Jake departed. I was told that such connections following the death of a loved one are not uncommon at all. Too many hypnagogic events occurred in the weeks and months following Jake's passing for me to dismiss or deny what was happening. I was never so unsure of myself and life yet eerily at ease with this energy force that kept me ethereally connected to Jake. When they did occur, the experiences were addicting, and I would find myself craving more signs, most especially when too much time passed between them. In those moments, a rare taste and touch of peace came over me, disrupting my mind from the everyday horror of my new existence.

My earliest childhood memories involved sports. Everything was sports. If I wasn't playing one, I was glued to the television consuming the action and analysis, studying and dissecting it, yearning to apply the knowledge to my own games. I played and loved all sports, but football, in particular college football, held a special place in my upbringing, high above all the others. My grandfather on my mother's side played on the 1930 freshman team at the University of Notre Dame (which happened to be coached by Knute Rockne). He graduated in 1934 and was later married on the campus. A framed photo of his freshmen team, which also included Moose Krause (who later became the athletic director at Notre Dame) and Hugh Devore (who went on to coach Notre Dame in 1945 and 1963, respectively), hangs in my home today. My grandfather's passion for his university and sport was injected into my veins. He exposed me to the rich and storied history of college football, including Notre Dame's place in it, and proudly modeled his devout loyalty to all things Fighting Irish.

Our bond was thickened on Saturday afternoons watching Notre Dame and other universities battle amid an unparalleled parade of pageantry and avidity. He regaled me with story after story, including several about the Gipper. I loved hearing about his experience and life on the campus, unconcerned about whether fable or fiction, and admired the depths of his fandom. He bled blue and gold; it openly oozed out of his pores. I carried that ardor and devotion forward in my life, consuming college football from coast to coast every Saturday in the fall. I used to walk around our home whistling random university fight songs I heard on television or the radio. In fact, it played a role in my decision to move to the South for college, where I could experience the sport I cherished on a deeper, more personal level in a region where the sport was revered. There's a truism in the South that there are only two sports: football and spring football.

But in the wake of losing Jake, the games suddenly meant nothing to me. I was uninspired and had no interest in even turning on the television to watch. What formerly had brought me much joy was now a lifeless experience. Grief erases joy like chalk on a blackboard.

Over a year passed before I experienced any return of joy while watching a college football game. But my perspective was undoubtedly altered. Our tragedy and its defiance of the natural order of things disturbed the lens from which I viewed everything. What once may have been a priority began to register as a trifle. The wins weren't as sweet, and the losses didn't sting nearly like before. They were just games, for God's sake, and in the big picture of life, there were more important and pressing matters than who won or lost a college football game.

The calendar now contains dates that I dread. Among them are Jake's birthday, May 13, August 9th, his high school graduation, the date all his friends left for college, parent's weekend at colleges and universities, the summer weeks leading up to and through August 9, and the entire holiday span from Thanksgiving through January 1, which represent a time when families happily gather and commune over food and football. For bereaved parents, none of that is possible. Someone very important is missing and his/her absence looms large over every occasion and milestone, most especially the annual ones.

I refuse to use the word "anniversary" to denote August 9. Rightly or wrongly, that word connotes a happier event than one used to honor the day someone died. Instead, I refer to it as a marker or the darkest day of the year, as if a pin was implanted into the wall calendar with permanent glue on that day. August 9 is and always will be the worst and longest day ever, one that I dread as it approaches and exhale the minute I make it through it, awakening to August 10.

As year one folded into year two, I found myself more capable of being reflective. I welcomed sitting in silence, most especially being outside in nature. I was told I looked better than before (before being six, eight, eleven months prior). Appearances can be deceiving. I was wracked with a shattered heart and a disrupted mind, a daily double no one desires. But no one could see that. I continued to immerse myself in stillness and books, everything from biographies to historical fiction to near-death stories and thought-provoking, spiritual reads. I read more books since losing Jake than in the combined decade before. Reading somehow proved to be a balm for my brain, offering both peace and a necessary distraction from darker thoughts. I watched documentaries and movies, reached out to an array of old friends and new friends, and leaned into my therapy to explore my unsettled place in this universe. It was suggested that I would one day be whole again and find a new purpose, but I would never be the same. And, if it was possible, year two was as painful, if not more, than year one, perhaps because I no longer had the benefit of shock protecting me from the tactility of the torturous life I led.

I sought clarity, if that was even possible, through self-reflection. I spent considerable time alone and deeply reviewed and explored my life, Jake's brief life, and the terrible event that forever changed our lives. What was I supposed to learn from this tragedy? What should or could I do about it? What did our future hold now? If something happened to Kellie and me, who would take care of Liam?

What I initially found through this process was that I was on edge and easily overwhelmed, waiting for another undesirable shoe to drop and on guard for every possible mishap that potentially could occur. I nearly had a panic attack the first time the three of us were together in a car driving on I-95. I became quickly staggered if too many things arose at once, whereas before, I thrived as a multitasker, seemingly capable of juggling sixteen balls in the air. Then, managing two things proved to be one too many. To this day, I am convinced I suffered some form of brain damage as a result of the acute trauma. My brain simply does not function like it did before August 9, 2020; it's slower, foggier, more forgetful, and disconnected in unexplainable ways. I became hypervigilant about my family's safety and well-being and utterly carefree, if not disconnected, from almost everything else.

I had very little energy and hoped that my dedication to slowing things down, spending more time alone, and reflecting might allow me to recharge and gain needed vitality. I was struggling through life and not enjoying very much of it. I said no to everything and anything I didn't feel up to doing and slowly began to write, mostly in the early, quiet morning hours when I was the only one awake in the darkness.

Writing, among other artistic pursuits, is encouraged for grievers. I was given multiple journals as condolence gifts (is there really such a thing?), which I initially tossed aside. I had no idea what to write about or where or how to start. Nor did I have any capacity for it. When I did begin to write many months later, it was sporadic, emotionally draining, and appeared as vomit on the paper. Run-on sentences, incongruent thoughts, and angry tones littered the pages.

I recall the first thing I wrote was a letter to Jake. I composed a string of paragraphs, writing as if he was away at camp, soon to return. I updated him on how much his mother, brother, and I missed him, and how proud of him we were, yet I stayed away from revealing the hurt we held or the reality that he was truly gone forever and would not be coming home. After that gut-wrenching exercise, I took a break from writing. Then, one morning, months later, I started again. Out of nowhere, I opened the laptop and slowly pecked away at the keyboard, one painful paragraph at a time. This process of self-exploration came with its own set of emotional releases and healthy respites before I could refuel, sit back down, and resume. I wrote, rewrote, deleted, cut and pasted, and moved paragraphs around. Initially, there was no agenda or purpose, just an innate urgency to eject some of the sorrow my overflowing body was holding onto.

"What we see depends mainly on what we look for," asserted Englishman John Lubbock. Have you ever struggled to complete a crossword puzzle? It can be frustrating. Have you stepped away from it for a period only to return with a completely different perspective? The answers to the clues, previously appearing unsolvable, now leap off the page. Likewise, stepping away from a dilemma and allowing time for reflection may point you toward a different mindset, leading to keen insights and, perhaps, a solution or new approach previously not contemplated. "The task is . . . not so much to see what no one has yet seen; but to think what nobody has yet thought, about that which everybody sees," counseled physicist Erwin Schrödinger.

You have the power to change your perspective. It will require patience and persistence, much reflection and risk. You may need to create new habits (which takes time) and pursue divergent avenues of thought or even gain invaluable third-party insight. You need to be willing to think innovatively and differently. "Often it isn't the mountains ahead that wear you out, it's the little pebble in your shoe," boldly pronounced Muhammed Ali. Don't get discouraged. It's never too late to evolve your approach to life, change a habit, or gain fresh, needed perspective.

How many times have you heard the phrase "life is short" before returning to your day-to-day minutiae? Life moves fast and only in one direction . . . forward. You can neither change the past nor truly predict the future. Yet time allows for self-reflection, where you may observe the footprints and missteps of your journey and learn from them. Contemplation expands awareness, enabling you to gain unforeseen insights you can apply moving . . . you guessed it . . . forward.

Here are three nuggets of life wisdom I derived from my personal self-reflection amid a background of darkness: First, live fully in the present moment. Looking backward or dreaming of the future is not active living. The late Buddhist monk, Thich Nhat Hanh, shared, "Many people are alive but don't touch the miracle of being alive." Time is the most precious commodity on earth. How do you choose to utilize the twenty-four hours of today? What happens is up to you to determine. It's a blank page waiting for you to write your story. Be the author of your memoir. Refuse to let someone else write it for you. Understand that there are no guarantees of tomorrow—and live like it. Don't take anything or anyone for granted. The things you may be taking for granted are those that others yearn for.

Second, the importance of laughter in life cannot be overstated. Laughter offers an array of positive healing and therapeutic benefits, including aiding resistance to disease. Charlie Chaplin famously said, "A day without laughter is a day wasted." Laughter can ease pain, relieve stress, and enhance your overall well-being. It may seem like an odd companion to grief, but I ultimately found laughter to be vital in feeling alive again. However, not before I encountered the most abnormal response to laughing for the first time in public, a mere three weeks after Jake's passing. We had out-of-town friends visiting, and they convinced us to go out for dinner one night—our first time out in public in such a setting. We agreed but desired to go out much later than normal to avoid being seen. Six of us arrived at a half-empty local establishment, its dining room slightly darkened as the host ushered us to a tucked-away table in a corner. At some point, one of our friends told a joke, and we all responded with uproarious laughter. It felt so good to laugh. But then I stopped and thought, *I'm not supposed to be laughing or happy, at least not in public*. It was such a peculiar, odd feeling but thankfully fleeting. Across the table, my eyes landed on Kellie, smiling and laughing for the first time since August 9. It was a beautiful sight to behold as I realized this was just what we needed: more laughter, lots of it, in fact, if we were ever going to make it out of hell. Abraham Lincoln famously quipped, "The fact is, I have always believed that a good laugh was good for both the mental and the physical digestion." Having lost a son of his own, eleven-year-old Willie, Lincoln later surmised, "I laugh because I must not weep—that's all, that's all."

Laugh with others and laugh at yourself. You may notice that laughter is contagious and a communal coping mechanism. It has the potential to conjoin friends with strangers and, equally, the power to diffuse tension and create intimacy. Laugh daily. Laugh often. Laugh loudly.

Third, at your primal core, love is why you are here. You are a social being and desire to be loved and emit love. The spiritual teacher Ram Dass captured the essence of love with this observation: "Unconditional love really exists in each of us. It is part of our deep inner being. It is not so much an active emotion as a state of being. It's not 'I love you' for this or that reason, not 'I love you if you love me.' It's love for no reason, love without an object." Love is much more than a simple feeling. It's a natural circumstance of being human, enabling you to crave it and desire to share it. It makes you act in ways that range from the pointless to the preposterous, irresponsible to idiotic, childish to crazy, and ridiculous to raw. Love can't be quantified, but it certainly can be communicated.

Jake loved music. Wherever he could be found—whether the shower, kitchen, beach, bus, or athletic field—music (often loud) always accompanied him. One of his favorite rappers, the late Juice Wrld, sang a line in one of his songs that depicts the unconditional love that Jake brought to this world: "This type of love don't always come and go."

As you move forward one day at a time, expand your perspective. Be mindful to enjoy the now. Laugh with frequency. Be generous and unconditional with your love. Your life is a string of moments. It's up to you to make them memorable.

Jake & Juice
© Jesse Lanham 2020

# Be it. Don't Talk it.

*"When you have confidence, you can have a lot of fun. And when you have fun, you can do amazing things."*

—Joe Namath

**WHILE THE ABOVE** quote is attributable to the brash, great quarterback known as Broadway Joe, its application far transcends the gridiron. Liam was a mere eleven years old when he lost his older brother and was compelled to traverse his unwanted grief journey. If I, an adult, struggled so mightily, how was a young boy supposed to process and move forward from the loss of his treasured older brother? I ached for him.

Liam revered his older brother despite being polar opposites in many regards. Jake was a natural athlete who loved sports. Liam wasn't as keen on participating in sports. Jake was an extrovert. Liam, an introvert. Jake preferred to lead, whereas Liam happily follows. Jake bonded immediately with people. Liam takes his time connecting. He's more deliberate and cautious.

They each beat to their own drummer. Jake's movements were faster, louder, and frenetic. Liam's pace is softer, more methodical. Jake's confidence was bold and omnipresent. Liam's is a work in progress but proves quiet when revealed. Jake loved the spotlight. Liam prefers the cover of camouflage and nightfall. Yet, both boys shared an empathetic and caring capacity, comfortable and at ease openly discussing their feelings.

Despite their different personalities and varied interests, their brotherly bond was one forged from mutual love and practical jokes. Jake challenged Liam, like most older brothers do, seeking to pass on his knowledge of the ways of the world. He also desired to influence Liam's musical tastes, improve his video game skills, and enhance his overall toughness. Jake was always available for Liam and loved to wrap his little brother in a bear hug.

It's been said that children who lose a sibling are the forgotten grievers. Adults and teachers are fearful of bringing up a sensitive subject, causing undue pain, and their peers aren't qualified to remotely touch the topic, wholly unsure of what to say or do. As a result, grieving children or siblings often go unattended. They have an uncanny ability to mask their pain and trauma, fooling everyone into mistakenly believing they are coping better than they actually are. They become hardened and strap on protective armor to bury their pain.

Liam was set to start the sixth grade three weeks after losing his brother. This meant moving from the elementary school building to the middle school, which shared the campus with the high school. Jake should have been next door to Liam, and Liam knew it. For the first six months of middle school, Liam soldiered through school and life. I honestly don't know how he did it. He rarely emoted and preferred to escape to his room to play video games and forget about how complex and screwed up our collective lives had just become. In the immediate weeks and months after August 9, 2020, Liam could often be found blaring Jake's playlist and singing along to the lyrics. I discovered a heartbreaking TikTok video he posted, exposing his sadness over losing his brother, where he emotionally narrated an ode to Jake over a slightly muffled song while a static picture of Jake and his girlfriend cuddling on our sofa flashed. To this day, Liam and I still listen to Jake's playlist on our drive to and from school each day.

In the fall of 2020, Liam, unprovoked by anyone other

than himself, returned to a team sport to honor Jake. He had previously tried flag football the year before but vowed never to return after an embarrassing incident in a game. One of the opposing defenders reached for Liam's flag as he ran with the ball, attempting to dodge oncoming tacklers. But the defender missed his flag and instead grabbed hold of Liam's shorts from behind, yanking them down to Liam's ankles in the middle of the field, leaving him exposed in his underwear. Liam was horrified and mad. We all joked that it was a good thing he had clean underwear on—or underwear at all. But he didn't find it as amusing as his teammates or us.

Yet, when offered the opportunity to return to flag football, Liam unabashedly stepped up. I couldn't have been prouder of him. A group of Jake's friends attended every one of his games, even arriving at the championship game with their chests painted in support of Liam.

Confidence is an aura and an energy. It can be quite palpable and is most certainly recognizable. Confidence can propel you to welcome new adventures and people into your life. It serves to motivate you to open doors even when you have no idea what's behind them. It inspires you to unconditionally believe in yourself and provokes a healthy sense of fearlessness.

That's exactly what happened to Liam. Over the two-year period from August 9, Liam doubled in weight and height, growing from a skinny little beanpole into Jake's sophomore clothes. Initially, it proved to be a very rough stretch for him. He was deeply lonely and lost without Jake. I related.

A change was needed, so we enrolled Liam in a new school for eighth grade, about twenty-five minutes away in a neighboring community. The class sizes were dramatically smaller, which provided a more supportive and welcoming approach. Liam was given a clean start at a place where the kids did not know that his brother had died. He wanted it that way, and frankly, I couldn't blame him. Jake's footprints loomed large, stretching far and wide. Attempting to live in the immense shadow of Jake was a tall order for anyone. Liam simply wanted to be Liam, a thirteen-year-old kid.

Liam was welcomed into his new school with open arms and big hearts. He quickly made friends and opted not to share his story of loss with anyone until halfway through the year, when he divulged the fact to his new best friend. Liam found his voice (now much deeper) and sense of self at school. He was heard, seen, loved, accepted, and coming alive again. He was maturing and growing in leaps and bounds, both physically and emotionally. He evolved from a stick figure into a confident, muscular teenager. He expressed interest in lifting weights and began playing basketball daily in our driveway.

Seeing Liam emerge from his grief with renewed confidence and a fresh smile provided a welcome relief for Kellie and me.

In some regards, it was as if Jake was filling Liam up with all the confidence he carried while with us. Whatever it was, we were grateful for his newfound confidence and zest for life. Liam was alive again—not just surviving but seeking to thrive.

Having confidence aids you in putting your failures and challenges into proper perspective, allowing you to take them in stride, learn from them, and hone your resilience muscle as you gain skills and coping methods. With self-confidence, you never lose sight of your ability to get the job done, no matter the obstacle. Confidence breeds respect, makes you less dependent on others, fosters your authenticity, and allows you to take decisive steps toward goals and dreams. "Confidence is contagious. So is lack of confidence," declared Vince Lombardi.

Self-confidence is further associated with not allowing "what-if" questions and thoughts to become paralyzing. Sometimes, it can be as simple as employing the counsel of Vincent van Gogh, who said, "If you hear a voice within you say 'you cannot paint,' then by all means paint, and that voice will be silenced." If you want others to believe in you, they must first accept that you believe in yourself.

Carrying yourself with a healthy swagger proclaims, *I can do this, and no one can stop me.* It's high-level confidence, direct and courage-filled, yet stops just short of being arrogant or abrasive. Arrogance, on the other hand, is simply an unsupported belief that you are better than others. Author and motivational speaker T. Harv Eker wrote, "Successful people have fear, successful people have doubts, and successful people have worries. They just don't let these feelings stop them."

It's been said that those who prevail believe they will. Dale Carnegie said it this way: "Inaction breeds doubt and fear. Action breeds confidence and courage. If you want to conquer fear, do not sit home and think about it. Go out and get busy." Present yourself with confidence. Expect the outcomes you desire. No one can stop you from reaching them but yourself. As Eleanor Roosevelt remarked, "No one can make you feel inferior without your consent."

Above all else: dream it, believe it, and achieve it.

You must conceive it to believe it. If you can do that, you will walk, talk, and live a life rife with confidence.

# Live Your Life in Harmony

*"Life is a balance of fear and overcoming it."*

—Jimmy Iovine

**BALANCE IS NOT** discovered by chance, rather it is something you manifest. It is dependent on what you think, how you carry yourself, and whether you can let go of things. There's only so much a human body can carry, physically and emotionally. What you prioritize matters.

Whether you achieve balance is often determined by whether you allow your heart and mind to synchronize. You have likely heard the phrase "everything in moderation," but have you pragmatically implemented it? Once you do so, you will discover the pathway toward leading a more balanced and fulfilling life. Too much of any one thing or feeling can tip the scales out of balance, leading to stress, anger, or emotions coming out sideways and in an unintended manner.

There are ways in which you can control your emotional balance. For example, when you feel dejected and sad, you can proactively choose to engage in a fun activity or intentionally seek out the companionship of a happy and optimistic friend to shake yourself out of a funk. You may also consider the practice of acknowledging the blessings in your life, which may just help balance the melancholy and provide you with a fresh, brighter mindset. Euripides wrote, "The best and safest thing is to keep a balance in your life, acknowledge the great powers around us and in us. If you can do that, and live that way, you are really a wise man."

Upon losing a child, there seemingly is no past, present, or future. Zero. Instead, there is one dark, cataclysmic, and starkly fatal state where you find yourself crouched over and helpless. It's impossible to move in any direction or accept the truth and what you will be forced to live without. Imbalance is an understatement. You don't feel strong or wise. You are paralyzed and powerless. One end of the seesaw of life is tipped downward, touching the ground, while the other points skyward and feels a million miles away, wholly out of balance.

Albert Einstein's genius is reflected in his proclamation that "life is like riding a bicycle. To keep your balance, you must keep moving." Grief seeks to hold you down. To re-achieve balance, you are required to punch, scratch, and crawl your way out from under the cloud of despair. I started with a focus on my physical and mental balance, believing I needed to be strong to feel strong and move forward one inch at a time.

I began exercising, stretching, and hiking. Daily rounds of push-ups, starting first thing in the morning, coupled with a yoga practice to stretch my discombobulated, inflexible body and stagnant mind, were the foundation. I needed to find a way to lighten the load and push beyond my fears, self-imposed boundaries, and quiet sorrow to release some of the pain my body was holding onto. This dedicated approach prioritized my well-being, shifting my focus toward self-care and renewing some semblance of balance in my life. As the weeks and months accumulated, I began to feel better about my ability to ultimately survive this horror.

For Christmas in 2022, I surprised Kellie and Liam with family boxing lessons at an old-school boxing gym. Every Friday evening, we wrap our hands, throw on boxing gloves, and beat the living hell out of a heavy bag. It's one of the most intensive, full-body workouts I have ever done. Simultaneously, we are being schooled in the technicalities of boxing's craft—keeping hands up, protecting the face and body, bobbing, weaving, dodging punches, and, imperatively, never standing still.

Not dissimilar from life, balance in boxing is critical, often proving to be the difference between success and the agony of defeat. One of the first lessons you receive in boxing focuses on your stance. Having a solid foundation that keeps your body stable and balanced empowers you to be in a position to attack as well as defend. As you weave, bob, and move around, it's vital that you are grounded. You accomplish this by ensuring your center of gravity is in harmony with your body movements.

In life, you must be mindful of how you arrange your foundation, positions, and time and how you manage expectations, boundaries, and priorities. While you are required to assess and alter how you oversee a day or week to attain a better life balance, what is more frequently required is a balance of your boundaries with people and your choices. Whether it's work-life or student-life balance, it's pivotal to include time for contemplation to allow for growth and context. Author Nishan Panwar concluded that "life is about balance. Be kind, but don't let people abuse you. Trust, but don't be deceived. Be content, but never stop improving yourself." While you strive for balance, there must be a recognition of how little you control. Focusing instead on the very few things you can control will greatly set you up for achieving balance and, ultimately, happiness in your life.

Never stop moving forward no matter what happens in your life.

Make your polestar positive.

Devote your energy toward creating balance.

# Look Life in the Face

*"The greatest test of courage on earth is to bear defeat without losing heart."*

—Robert G. Ingersoll

YOU AWAKE EACH day unaware of what life may or may not deliver to your doorstep. The impermanence of our existence is omnipresent. Yet it isn't until you're truly tested, challenged, or lose someone dear to you that you arrive face-to-face with the transient nature of human existence. In doing so, you will be challenged to discover the depths of your courage and belief in yourself to adapt and overcome hardship.

It is vital that you believe in yourself. If you don't, how can you reasonably expect anyone else to believe in you? Or support you and your goals and dreams? What is it that prevents you from having courage and self-confidence? Perhaps you allowed someone to convince you that you didn't possess what it takes. Or maybe it was your own self-created fear. Or, maybe, you lacked support from family and friends when you needed it most. Don't live a life in fear. Find a way, any way, to push through your fears, and you shall discover that your fortitude far exceeds any perceived fear.

No matter what it takes to surmount your own fears, keep in mind this German proverb: "Fear makes the wolf bigger than he is." When you realize that you are, in fact, capable of pushing past your own fears or overcoming a lack of support or indifference from others, you will begin to gain confidence, which fosters courage. It happens one small step at a time, no different than building a stone wall. Each stone is individually and methodically set in its proper place to ultimately amass the entire wall, one stone atop another, atop another. Likewise, each instance of conquering a single fear leads to another moment of building up resilience to other fears. Nelson Mandela's perspicacious intuition led him to share this: "I learned that courage was not the absence of fear but the triumph over it. The brave man is not he who does not feel afraid but he who conquers that fear."

Fears surround you, whether perpetuated by others, society, or yourself. We all have something we likely fear or that holds us back in some manner. But have you ever just stopped and thought, *What's the worst thing that could happen if I push through the fear?* When you honor that you possess the ability to push through self-imposed boundaries and overcome fear, you will be inspired to drop any future veil of fear and adopt the spirit of courage, the spirit of fearlessness. Don't waste another hour or day allowing a life setback, challenge, or obstacle to devour you. The ability and power source to conquer this resides within you. You just need to locate and deploy it. Admittedly, it's not always easy. But then again, nothing of meaning is.

When you lose a child, your fears, large and small, are magnified on an unimaginable scale. You become hypervigilant in ways you never were before. The first time we allowed Liam to get into someone else's vehicle after losing Jake made us swallow very hard. More than a few slight traces of fear entered our minds. How could they not? I also found myself driving slower than ever when operating a car. I cringed when I heard sirens and winced whenever I saw an ambulance speeding and lights flashing, undoubtedly en route to save a life. I jumped when horns were honked or unexpected loud sounds occurred.

This behavior was foreign to me. I despised feeling anxious and being on edge. I nearly puked on myself one day when compelled to stop at a green traffic light to allow a passing hearse and a subsequent, steady procession of cars slowly advancing toward a cemetery. I worried about those very few occasions when Kellie left the house. My mind raced with worst-case scenarios. In many respects, if you don't channel courage, you may become immobilized by your fears.

When I took my first out-of-town work trip nineteen months into my grief, I had to coordinate a detailed schedule of family and friends to watch over Kellie and Liam in my absence. I was off to New Orleans, the city where Jake was born, headed straight for the epicenter where the memories commenced. I was aware that I was about to be triggered in a dramatic manner and would need to conjure up the inner strength to surf the epic waves of grief that would undoubtedly cascade over me.

As the airplane began its descent, I glanced out the window and recognized so many familiar sights and old-stomping grounds. *Here came the first wave,* I thought as a series of early recollections of living in New Orleans with young Jake washed over me: from his birth during a darker-than-normal evening that carried with it strong winds and even a tornado warning, carrying him in the BabyBjörn during Mardi Gras, his baptism, which occurred on the Magnolia bridge spanning Bayou St. John (a place where Jake took his first steps and learned to walk), and all the other places we brought him, which was seemingly everywhere we went. The airplane hadn't even touched down yet, and I was wiping away bittersweet tears.

I don't recall when or how things changed. In fact, I can't recall very much of anything from the first year of my grief. Writer and filmmaker Nora Ephron advised that "above all, be the heroine of your life, not the victim." But somehow, with time, my capacity for courage trumped the fears that pervaded me. Who wants to live in fear? Not me. It's a terrible state to find yourself in, beyond frightening, and completely unhealthy. Surrendering to the fact that there was nothing I could have done to save Jake on that fateful day played an instrumental role in my transformation from fear to fortitude. I moved past self-directed guilt, shame, or blame. Yes, we are collateral damage from that tragedy and suffer more than anyone, but I refused to be a victim or remain benumbed by circumstances outside my control. I also no longer feared my death.

Why allow anyone else, an internal claim, or an external unfounded claim to dictate your story or life? Uncover your courage; it's there waiting for you. Despite whatever occurs in your journey, never lose heart and faith in yourself. Scottish novelist Robert Louis Steven sensibly counseled "keep your fears to yourself, but share your courage with others."

Admittedly, being courageous isn't always effortless. In fact, the road to courage and fearlessness is far from paved or direct. You will need to discover your true heart and listen to your inner voice to reveal and source your courage. But if you are willing to be brave enough to try, the rewards are limitless. T.S. Eliot concluded "only those who will risk going too far can possibly find out how far one can go." What are you willing to risk to get what you want?

# Be Hungry for the Experience in Your Journey

*"Life is the art of drawing without an eraser."*

—John W. Gardner

**EVERY WAKING MOMENT** is an experience. Are you participating in each moment? Do you have your eyes wide open, and are you alert enough to see the opportunities and new pathways being offered to you? Or are you moving through life so fast and furiously that you allow experiences to pass you by? Or worse, are you so numb and closed off to this existence that you are relegated to the role of silent spectator? Poet Emily Dickinson imparted, "The soul should always stand ajar, ready to welcome the ecstatic experience."

You can embrace, accept, or reject what you see, feel, read, touch, and hear. Equally, you are capable of discovering the truth and essence of a debate, distinguishing what matters from the rubbish, and ascertaining what works from that which has no shot of making a difference. "Experience is simply the name we give our mistakes," wrote Oscar Wilde. Making mistakes is both a part of your life and a stepping stone toward building, conquering doubt, and achieving dreams. Self-doubt often exists until you try something yourself. You can spectate all you want, but until you jump into the arena of life and fully participate in a hands-on experience, you will never know how that experience makes you feel, what it can provide you, or understand the nuances involved. Be open to tasting the adventure of life, which undoubtedly comes with spiced peaks and sweet valleys.

President Harry S. Truman surmised, "The reward of suffering is experience." When I originally shared that quote with Jake when he was a mere nine years old, it meant something different to both of us. Like many things in life, context matters greatly. Today, it's much harder to swallow Truman's counsel. No human would ever agree to accept losing their child for whatever (new) experience stemmed from it. Trust me, there is nothing pleasant about this experience. Zero. Nada. This experience leaves you with a gaping hole in your heart, which you are compelled to carry all the way to your final breath. There is absolutely no reward. Instead, there is an empty bedroom and an unimaginable void and pain. Only three places are set for dinner now, and only three stockings hang at Christmas in our home. When we go out to eat, the hostess asks, "How many are you?" The answer is a sad and hollow, "Three."

Buddhists subscribe to four noble truths, the first of which proclaims, "life is suffering (dukkha)." One definition of dukkha is all that is temporary and conditional. There is a beginning and end to everything—seasons, careers, moments, and life. Whether bad or good, everything comes and goes. You understand and accept that each passing day is one step closer to your death. Whether you admit it or not, you're living your life to a shot clock ticking away time with each inhale. Impermanence surrounds us, but we rarely talk about it. It's too dark and dreary. Maybe it should openly be discussed more. If it were, you just might live your life with a greater sense of urgency, compassion, and love for one another. Your appetite for every experience that crosses your path might be considerably larger and more open and your appreciation for connecting with people who orbit your world keener and more welcoming.

As difficult as it is to write this, I have surrendered to the possibility that maybe, just maybe, Jake wasn't supposed to be on this planet for very long. Perhaps it's just a coping mechanism I've embraced so I don't drive myself insane chasing the "why." He lived in a way that suggested that was the case, doing and being more than most of us can in a full life. All I know for sure is that I will never get him back. I will never feel the strong embrace of a Jake bear hug. I will never attend another college football game with him. I will never hear him tell a funny story or joke. I will never hear him sing in the shower. I will never watch another movie with him. I will never see him attend and graduate from college. I will never hear his magnificent laugh. I will never see him fall in love and get married. I will never get the opportunity to see how beautiful his children would have been and what an amazing father he would have become. That is the somber fate of a bereaved parent—a life of never agains.

While a part of each of us died with Jake, a part of him remains in each of our souls, allowing him to experience what we continue to experience. We take him everywhere we go. Jake and Kellie were incredibly close, kindred spirits, you might say. This makes sense since she knew him nine months before I did—the benefit of a mother's experience of carrying the child inside her belly, connected in the most primal of ways. She was more than his food source. Their souls are forever linked. The bond between a mother and her children is undeniably robust and everlasting. Jake and Kellie had an uncanny way of thinking the same thing at the exact same time and pursuing joy and laughter at every turn.

The joy is diminished, and the laughter is less, but I like to think that the reward of suffering is the reward of living; it's up to you whether a singular experience can defeat you or whether you instead choose to move forward and experience the wholeness of life. As author Kevin Kelly shared in *Excellent Advice for Living:*

*Wisdom I Wish I'd Known Earlier*, "Bad things can happen fast but almost all good things happen slowly."

You must seize the adventures offered to you in life. It is the most profound and meaningful way to evolve and grow. Philosopher Albert Camus intelligently offered, "You cannot create experience. You must undergo it." Are you actively living or passively observing? Take advantage of the diversity of people and experiences that will cross your path and arrive at your feet. By doing so, you will avail yourself of new understandings and keen insights. Your journey will be more enriched by absorbing the cruelty of life and continuing in a manner in which you are more receptive to the greater good of humanity. Comedian Steven Wright joked that "experience is something you don't get until just after you need it." Don't waste another day living with your eyes shut. Live curiously, open to acquiring knowledge, evolving your thinking, and conquering your challenges.

Be brave. Take risks. Welcome each experience in your life with joy. Win the day!

Kellie & Jake on his sixteenth birthday

# The Pursuit of Happiness

*"The most worthwhile thing is to try and put happiness into the lives of others."*

—Robert Baden-Powell

**THERE IS NO** singular pathway leading to happiness. Every person's journey toward fulfillment and the pursuit of happiness is deeply personal and a universal quest spanning the globe. Reverend John B. Sheerin, a pioneer in interfaith relations, said, "Happiness is not in our circumstances, but in ourselves. It is not something we see, like a rainbow, or feel, like the heat of a fire. Happiness is something we are."

For some, happiness is unachievable. Likely because they are looking for it in places or things that won't result in a state of bliss. It isn't derived from material things or singular moments, rather the focus must be inward in order to discover your true, natural happiness. Stop chasing the artificial, fleeting, filtered, and overedited. Your happiness transcends a momentary mood. Rather "happiness . . . is a quality of thought, a state of mind," wrote novelist Daphne du Maurier. You certainly experience both positive and negative emotions in your daily life, and your ability to regulate those ever-fluctuating emotions plays a crucial role in determining your overall happiness. English essayist Joseph Addison proposed that "the grand essentials to happiness in this life are something to do, something to love, and something to hope for."

Jake was born happy, a blessing bestowed upon him by God. He exuded joy and spread love like a card dealer at a blackjack table. I was driving Liam to school one morning in the fall of 2022 when, out of the blue, Liam said, "Dad, I'm trying to be more like Jake. He had fun in everything he did and with everyone. I'm not Jake, but I can certainly try to live like he did." I nodded, looked at Liam, smiled, and replied, "Yes, Jake set a high bar for how to live a happy life." And then I turned up the volume on the radio, and we returned to listening to Jake's playlist.

Jake's friends, who spent the final morning of his life with him hanging out on the beach on Block Island, recalled that they had never seen him happier. He enthusiastically shared with them his plan to attend the University of South Carolina upon graduating high school in 2022. He knew what he wanted and where he wanted to go next. For Jake, happiness was as essential as oxygen, and he found his joy in living fully, loving everyone, and hoping for more, much more, of it all.

If you're happy, your relationships, health, and career may stand to gain. "The happiest people are those who are too busy to notice whether they are or not," sensibly pointed out publisher and editor William Feather. The benefits of happiness are not limited to just you. Your happiness increases the likelihood of your participation and contributions within your community. "In about the same degree as you are helpful, you will be happy," commanded the Rev. Dr. Karl Reiland. There's your reason to make a positive impact. Spread happiness to others.

Did you know that happiness is contagious? The ripple effect of happiness can emanate from a single individual (you!) and impact many, according to a study conducted by researchers from Harvard University and the University of California, San Diego. The best way to spread happiness is through the authentic display of care and concern for others. Try it today. Do something nice for someone. I dare you. "Make one person happy each day and in forty years you will have made 14,600 human beings happy for a little time, at least," smartly recommended Charley Willey.

I believe Jake's spirit remains as happy and bright as he was living on earth. There is no end to the positive influence and impact he will forever have on the communities he continues to touch. The aura of his love and light will forever shine. Thankfully, I continue to bear witness to it.

It was up to me, and only me, to rediscover happiness in the face of grief. In time, my inner happiness rejected the remnants of anguish. Standing still in gloom wasn't an option. Moving forward and accepting what few things were within my control was the only way out. "Happiness consists not in having much, but in being content with little," said Irish novelist Lady Marguerite Blessington.

Stop looking around for your happiness. It lies within you.

Jake and Liam, July 2016

# Be Great Together

*"What divides us pales in comparison with what unites us."*

—Edward Kennedy

**AS A CHILD**, did you play the game King of the Mountain?

The goal is to ascend the mountain, standing alone on top. Getting there, however, isn't easy. It's every person for themselves—a complete free-for-all. Once you reach the top, everyone tries to throw you off. The worst place to be, actually, is alone on top. You find yourself paranoid, unable to trust anyone, constantly spinning and attempting to guard every direction. You become so consumed with defending your back—no one else is watching it for you—that you can't relax and enjoy the view from the peak of the mountain.

As you mature, the game and the mountain evolve into and represent something much bigger in your life: a sport, season, career, relationship, or more. And being at the apex by yourself is lonely and can make you feel powerless rather than powerful.

The reality is that instead of forging ahead as a singular person and fighting everyone for the top of the mountain, recognize that there's more power ascending together as a team. There is a sacred and shared purpose in the pain of the climb. "On or off the field, practice and teamwork are the key to success," offers two-time Super Bowl champion Malcolm Jenkins.

It's good to have individual goals, but don't get trapped into thinking those individual goals trump the team or relationship goals. "Teamwork requires some sacrifice up front; people who work as a team have to put the collective needs of the group ahead of their individual interests," writes Patrick Lencioni, author of *The Five Dysfunctions of a Team*, a popular business fable that explores teamwork dynamics. Likewise, any healthy relationship requires compromise, along with common effort and agreement.

"The strength of the team is each individual member. The strength of each member is the team," observantly offered eleven-time NBA champion coach Phil Jackson. The success of a team or relationship will empower you and your teammates or colleagues. You will inspire and love each other along the way. When one is down, another will lift them up. A culture is vigorous and durable when people collaborate with each other and for each other.

This brotherhood or sisterhood mentality is about fellowship and empowerment. "There is a destiny which makes us brothers; none goes his way alone. All that we send into the lives of others comes back into our own," wrote poet Edwin Markham. You can be vulnerable and connect with one another in a way that allows for understanding, respect, and mutual accountability. By leaning on others, a fresh perspective may be illuminated. The only way through and beyond hardships is to stick together as one.

I have been supported by an array of amazing friends and family over the last several years. While I understood it was up to me and me alone to take steps forward, there is little question that I would never have achieved it without the unconditional love and support of so many. Whether it was a pop-in visit offering encouragement or simply an ear, a phone call, someone mowing my lawn unannounced, the gift of a book or an invitation to hang out over a beer, or meal after meal being brought to our home for months on end, people stepped up at a time of great need, revealing the beauty in humanity. "Develop a sense of the brotherhood of man. Look upon each person as your own brother. There is only one caste, the caste of humanity. All of us belong to the human race, so everyone is equal. Therefore, love each one equally," decreed Indian guru Sathya Sai Baba.

When you finally ascend to the top of your mountain, arriving at the pinnacle as one, you will have others to celebrate and share it with. You won't fret defending your back because your teammates, friends, brothers, and sisters will have your back. You'll be focused on who to hug and celebrate with. Together, you will share the most breathtaking view and memories of your collective journey in rising as one through the collaborative spirit of teamwork.

Helen Keller may have said it best: "Alone we can do so little. Together we can do so much." We are all connected, part of one tribe, so let's start behaving like it.

# Enthusiasm Is Contagious

*"You can do anything if you have enthusiasm. Enthusiasm is the yeast that makes your hopes rise to the stars."*

—Henry Ford

**ARE YOU LIVING** your life with excitement and enthusiasm? Or are you opting to sit in the back of the car, allowing others to steer your life, leaving you an uninspired observer? Don't be a dull passenger in life. English poet and writer L.E. Landon penned, "Enthusiasm is the divine particle in our composition; with it we are great, generous, and true; without it, we are little, false, and mean."

Who are you more likely to pick as your work or team partner? The person who has no energy, is satisfied with mediocrity, and lacks passion? Or the one whose energy, enthusiasm, and fervor bubbles out of their pores? An enthusiastic person stimulates every single person around them, leading to anticipation of greater things. They are engaging and often a driving force in compelling a deeper exploration of self. Being around people with ardor and optimism is infectious and can be the difference between winning and losing, getting the job or not, or success or disappointment. Vince Lombardi famously quipped, "If you aren't fired with enthusiasm, you will be fired with enthusiasm."

You should surround yourself with people who inspire you with their drive and enthusiasm, allowing their energy to spill onto you. You must discover what is important in your life and what you are good at. When you do, your passion will be revealed, and more fun will be injected into the process of your pursuits. Who doesn't want more fun in their life? Malcolm Forbes once wisecracked, "People who never get carried away should be."

Positivity and enthusiasm also serve you well during life's more challenging moments. "Adversity causes some men to break, others to break records," noted motivational scribe William A. Ward. A positive conviction not only breeds confidence but is also essential to advancement and achievement. "The only thing that keeps a man going is energy. And what is energy but liking life?" posed Louis Auchincloss.

Therein lies the essential fork in the road of grief. One road presents life, albeit much different than what you knew before. The other road offers more despair. A common question posed to grievers is one I heard, too. "What would Jake want for you?" Then the questioner would, without hesitation, answer their own question. "He would want you to be happy, to live your life fully, and to make a difference in the lives of others." It was mere weeks into my grief when I first heard this. Naturally, I dismissed it with haste. How do you know what Jake would want? Jake would want to be here with us. Jake would never, ever, want to cause this kind of pain for his mother, brother, or me, I contended. It was not his nature.

My defiance was based on my anger about our circumstances. In an instant, our lives were shattered, and the future appeared bleak. A friend once told me, "Time is the ultimate quaalude." Well, making space and time for confronting my grief head-on required me to accommodate for an inordinate amount of contemplation, time spent in nature, and escaping our home through frequent weekend getaways. Ultimately, I was able to reclaim my enthusiasm by honoring Jake's life in a variety of ways, the least of which was awarding scholarships to children who now carry a part of Jake with them as they pursue their aspirations.

It is absolutely necessary that your enthusiasm and energy be nourished and inspired through the cycle of new ideas, people, and dreams. We all should heed Watterson Lowe's learned counsel: "Years wrinkle the face, but to give up enthusiasm wrinkles the soul." We all take for granted that we will live long enough to experience wrinkles. However, it's the depth and breadth of living a life filled with enthusiasm—not the years—that fuels us.

Make your life exciting and not a chore. Bring to it an unrivaled passion and enthusiasm.

You don't get to decide how you die. But you have a say in how you live. Do it with enthusiasm.

# Family Ties/Friendships Matter

*"A real friend is one who walks in when the rest of the world walks out."*

—Walter Winchell

**FAMILY MAY BE** the institution that you draw the most meaning from, mainly because you are compelled to spend significant time during your formative years with them, resulting in an understanding of your idiosyncrasies, habits, quirks, and desires. They also come to learn your imperfections and foibles, and you theirs. "Call it a clan, call it a network, call it a tribe, call it a family. Whatever you call it, whoever you are, you need one," wrote novelist Jane Howard.

From an early age, a healthy family is there to support and love you. It can provide a sense of belonging and identity, aid you in modeling right and wrong behaviors, and shape your beliefs and expectations early in life. "Other things may change us, but we start and end with the family," opined composer Anthony Brandt. Unfortunately, not everyone is blessed with a healthy family structure. Unhealthy standards, habits, and models also exist.

In our home, everyone had the right to call a "family meeting" at any time. Both Jake and Liam frequently called meetings. We all convened on two sofas that faced one another. The person calling the meeting would reveal what was on their mind, which sparked a conversation, debates, and often understanding and healing. We were compelled to intently listen to whoever had the floor, and when they were done, we were given ample time to reply and respond.

Our family meetings were Kellie's idea. It was a truly brilliant notion, as our boys learned to hone their communication skills. They became better listeners, developed a greater sense of empathy, and learned to value input and constructive criticism from others. Differences were healed, and dysfunction was limited through our family meetings. But not every meeting required an issue to be fixed. Sometimes, we convened just to check in with one another, hear what was going on in each person's world, or laugh and connect over a lighthearted matter.

I will always fondly remember one specific family meeting that spawned out of the boredom of being cooped up inside the house during the early COVID-19 period. Needing a break from watching Netflix, we decided to do impersonations of one another. Kellie went first and mocked me. The boys roared with laughter. Then Jake hilariously mimicked Liam and his occasional stubbornness that stalled family activities from time to time. Liam then posed as me, acting like he couldn't find something that was literally right under his nose while asking everyone if they saw it or knew where it was. We all bent over in laughter.

Then it was my turn. I retreated to the kitchen, grabbed Kellie's purse, threw it over my arm, sashayed back into the room, and lambasted the boys for not coming out to the driveway to help carry the groceries, loudly proclaiming, "There are too many boys in this house. I need a girl!"—a line that Kellie would utter when frustrated as the only woman in the house. I will never forget the uncontrollable laughter that poured out of Jake. He couldn't stop. Those are the moments and memories that stay with you. I will forever cherish those family times.

Family of Four, October 2019

As you mature, leave home, and proceed on your journey, your family often remains your bedrock of support. Whether a phone call, flight, or short walk away, the unconditional ear and love of a family member provides security and stability.

Yet, families are far from perfect and equally the source of conflicts, misunderstandings, disagreements, splinters, drama, and more. It isn't realistic to believe that all relationships, family or otherwise, will always be harmonious and easy. Dysfunction runs rife in healthy and unhealthy family dynamics. But you learn to hone your interpersonal conflict resolution skills first and foremost inside the dynamic of the family circle. Through his unique comedic nature, George Carlin offered this up about families: "The other night I ate at a real nice family restaurant. Every table had an argument going."

How you maneuver such periods of strife and evolve as a family will ultimately be determined by your response to each situation. As author Jim Butcher half-jokingly identified, "There's nothing that makes you more insane than family. Or more happy. Or more exasperated. Or more . . . secure." Butcher concluded, "When everything goes to hell, the people who stand by you without flinching—they are your family." In the end, comedian Les Dawson reminds us that "families are like fudge—mostly sweet, with a few nuts."

Your close friends may feel like family or even closer than family. You can say anything to a close friend, and they accept it. You can also typically work through any issues with a dear friend with ease and a level of mutual understanding. Ralph Waldo Emerson wrote, "It is one of the blessings of old friends that you can afford to be stupid with them." You don't get to pick your family, but you possess the right to select and hone your friendships.

Friendships can be lifelong endeavors—bonds supported by admiration, intimacy, respect, and trust. They may further aid you in your discovery of purpose and meaning, serving as a sounding board to your thoughts and ideas and a mirror to your actions. "There is no wilderness like a life without friends; friendship multiplies blessings and minimizes misfortunes; it is a unique remedy against adversity, and it soothes the soul," advised Baltasar Gracian. Other friendships may serve a time, place, or station in your life, which is normal.

Your time spent with family contrasts with time spent with friends. Family events may become plodding and routine or carry with them different expectations as they annually appear on your calendar. Friendship gatherings, on the other hand, may offer spontaneity, diversity, and less stress. "Friends are the family we choose for ourselves," offered Edna Buchanan.

Not dissimilar from many things in life, friendships take effort and work to succeed and grow. "One of the most beautiful qualities of true friendship is to understand and to be understood," counseled Lucius Annaeus Seneca. What you put into your friendships is often, though not always, what you receive back. Are you truly available to sit with a friend and listen to what's going on in their life? Do you make time to catch up? Are you comfortable being vulnerable with a friend, sharing your deeper, innermost thoughts and hearing theirs? Are you there for each other, whenever and wherever the need or time arises to support one another?

Affirmative answers reveal the depths, bonds, and reciprocity of your friendships. "No medicine is more valuable, none more efficacious, none better suited to the cure of all our temporal ills than a friend to whom we may turn for consolation in times of trouble, and with whom we may share our happiness in time of joy," suggested Saint Aelred of Rievaulx.

The ideal way to make and sustain a positive, healthy, and long-term friendship is to simply be an authentic friend. "The language of friendship is not words but meanings," wrote Henry David Thoreau. How and with whom you cultivate friendships impacts your overall happiness and arguably your success. "Lots of people want to ride with you in the limo, but what you want is someone who will take the bus with you when the limo breaks down," proposed Oprah Winfrey. True friendships make you better. And much is revealed by the circle of friends you choose to surround yourself with.

Appreciate your family and relish your friends.

# Two Ears, One Mouth

*"Friends are those rare people who ask how we are, and then wait to hear the answer."*

—Ed Cunningham

I WAS RAISED in rural, upstate New York, land of the Iroquois, a confederacy of five tribes—Cayuga, Onondaga, Seneca, Oneida, and Mohawk. As such, it was no coincidence that I was instructed from an early age with the wisdom of the Iroquois: "The Great Spirit gave you two ears and only one mouth, so you can talk half as much as you listen."

Listening is a conscious effort to give your full and undivided attention to another, such that you fully comprehend, and not just hear, what the other person is saying or sharing with you. It requires patience, concentration, and often a healthy dose of focus. As cartoonist Frank Tyger wisecracked, "Be a good listener. Your ears will never get you in trouble."

Numerous university-led studies have examined the ability to effectively listen. They have all generally reached the same conclusion: the average person remembers only about one-half of what they have heard immediately following a short talk. How can you expect to be successful or even trusted if you only hear half of what someone is telling you?

You were taught how to read, instructed in persuasive writing skills, and perhaps even trained how to speak a foreign language.

Yet not a single listening class was offered despite the awareness that once you enter the real world, you will listen three times more than you read. I find this fundamental communication imbalance astounding, explaining why so many disconnections, strife, and worse occur daily, all because of a lack of listening.

The benefits of being a good listener are vast and desirable. Listening helps avoid misunderstandings and reduces the potential for conflicts. It helps enhance friendships, advance business and professional relationships, and promote healthy romantic relationships and marriages. It deepens trust and fosters successful leadership skills.

Listening is pivotal in grief. We would have been lost without our grief therapist's compassion, wisdom, and ear. His ability to empathetically weave and maneuver through our deep pain and frequent tears saved us. His provocative insights built bridges of survival between our twice-weekly sessions. The key was actively listening to him and each other.

Despite that Kellie and I shared grief over losing Jake, our pathways were uniquely disparate. We emoted differently and at contrasting times. The grief experience for men and women is wholly divergent. Everyone has heard the phrase "men are from Mars, women from Venus." Not shockingly, it's applicable in grief as well. We shared some emotional triggers yet were conflicted with our individual, haunting ones. We checked in with each other frequently, lifted the other up, and shared "nuggets" of wisdom learned along the way. We intently listened and respected feelings and nightmares. It was the only way to survive together.

Author and thought leader Bryant H. McGill proposed, "One of the most sincere forms of respect is actually listening to what another has to say." Do you *hear* someone, or are you *listening*? Hearing requires no effort and is automatic. You naturally hear background noise, voices, birds, phones, dishwashers, and cars.

Conversely, listening is a skill where effort, focus, and motivation are mandatory. To listen is to be active, display care, and truly embrace what the other needs or wants to share. You may not agree, but what's the harm in truly listening?

Have you ever noticed that you are able to close your mouth but not your ears?

When you listen, you learn!

# Forgiveness Is Healing

*"The weak can never forgive.
Forgiveness is the attribute of the strong."*

—Mahatma Gandhi

**IMAGINE IF SOMEONE** asked you to hold a twenty-pound bag of cement for twenty minutes. Your arms would likely grow tired, and your body would become tense, drained, and exhausted from bearing the added weight. The cement unquestionably is unwieldy, weighs you down, and seemingly feels heavier with each passing minute. Yet releasing it frees you from stress and a burden. Metaphorically, that's not dissimilar to what occurs when you opt to hold onto anger or a grudge rather than letting it go. When you find forgiveness in your heart, you release anger. "Forgiveness is man's deepest need and highest achievement," preached Horace Bushnell, a Congregational minister and theologian. The longer you hold onto anger, the more cumbersome it becomes, weighing you down and limiting joy, enthusiasm, and overall happiness.

The act of forgiving is transformational, liberating you from past suffering. Author and theologian Lewis B. Smedes aptly described it this way: "To forgive is to set a prisoner free and discover that the prisoner was you." Don't you wish to suffer less? I know I do. Letting go of past pain is an immense step toward making your life lighter, brighter, and more fulfilling.

And it begins with you. "Letting ourselves be forgiven is one of the most difficult healings we will undertake. And one of the most fruitful," counseled Stephen Levine, highly regarded author and teacher on death and dying.

The hard truth is that when a child dies, a natural feeling surfaces—an inner desire to blame something or someone for your loss. You feel victimized. The natural order of life has been turned on its head, and anger and frustration link hand in hand with shock and trauma. There are no rules in grief. Your body undergoes a complete and utter disruption. You can't think, let alone contemplate, with any sense of logic or order. Forgiveness simply is not top of mind. Nobody ever claimed it's easy and effortless to forgive, most especially when consumed by grief and when you feel utterly victimized and violated by the universe.

If it was uncomplicated, the planet would be filled with more love than anger, more peace than strife, and more harmony than discord. The profound reaction and emotions I experienced upon losing Jake will never go away; it's seared into my muscle memory and runs deep in my veins. "One forgives to the degree that one loves," claimed French moralist Francois de La Rochefoucauld. When you make the conscious decision to let go and free yourself by forgiving, you experience inner freedom and arrive at a place of peace over your loss, shedding anger and angst. Renowned poet William Blake eloquently provided this visual illustration and perspective on the power of forgiveness when he wrote, "Even the cut worm forgives the plow." Admittedly, it's a process and takes some time. But once you understand the power of forgiveness, your direction is obvious.

Acclaimed poet Maya Angelou wrote, "It's one of the greatest gifts you can give yourself, to forgive. Forgive everybody." Importantly, forgiveness doesn't necessarily mean dismissing the past or pain. Nor does it mean that the wrongdoer isn't held accountable or that you can't establish healthy boundaries to avoid future suffering. Forgiveness is about you, not them. You are choosing to be powerful rather than powerless, and, ultimately, to recognize that you control your choices, not theirs. "The moment an individual can accept and forgive himself, even a little, is the moment in which he becomes to some degree lovable," psychologist Eugene Kennedy advocated. When you forgive, you reclaim your life. Letting go and moving on is your choice—the best avenue for growth and healing.

Undoubtedly, you have been forgiven by someone along the way. If God will forgive you, why shouldn't you forgive another? "The truth is, unless you let go, unless you forgive yourself, unless you forgive the situation, unless you realize that the situation is over, you cannot move forward," said Steve Maraboli. Don't allow your past the power to control your present.

Learning to move forward while also integrating and carrying grief is weighty enough. The minute I finished delivering the speech and awarding Matthew Bailey with the inaugural Jake Panus Walk On Scholarship, I realized I no longer needed to carry the extra bag of cement. Instead, when Matthew embraced me in a hug, surprised and grateful for his scholarship, I found myself letting go and opening my fractured but still pulsating heart to our connection, which was based upon mutual pure love, appreciation, and gratitude. I walked away from that meeting of the hearts still in pain yet filled with a renewed purpose.

I refuse to allow my being, thoughts, or actions to be further polluted by offenders and events outside my control. Instead, I have chosen to forgive everyone involved in the senseless and tragic events of August 9, 2020, in order to *walk on* in my life.

Jake, October 2019

Jake, May 2019

# Epilogue

IN 2010, I took a memorable road trip across the country with Jake, who was six years old. We were in the midst of a family relocation from Las Vegas back to the Northeast. Because Liam was a one-year-old, Kellie and Liam traveled by airplane ahead of us. Jake and I had the luxury of not being restrained by any deadlines, and with our dog happily in the back seat, we decided to make an adventure out of it. We laid out a map and charted an unconventional course that focused on landmarks rather than highways. It would eventually take us from the desert to the mountains, the prairies to the Midwest, before eventually landing in the overpopulated Northeast corridor.

One of our favorite places was the Little Bighorn National Monument in Montana. The landscape was breathtaking. Undulating hills rolled one over another, and the tall, wispy green, golden grass and sagebrush swayed back and forth with each passing breeze. White marble gravestones, some perfectly aligned in row after row and others sporadically placed where soldiers actually fell to their deaths, were sprinkled across the grassy hillside. They denoted the many interred soldiers whose lives ended that fateful day. The Native American warriors were honored by red-speckled granite memorial markers which dotted the rolling hillsides for their part in the Battle of Greasy Grass.

The unmistakable energy from that historic battle seemingly still spun in the gusts of winds that hovered across and amid the naturally beautiful scenery.

We also visited Yellowstone National Park and the Badlands National Park in South Dakota, among other stops. The drive from Chicago, where we briefly stayed with family, to the Northeast paled in comparison to our time in Montana, Wyoming, and South Dakota, places Lewis and Clark described as "scenes of visionary enchantment."

A short while after arriving and settling into our new home, one of my aunts encouraged me to see a psychic medium that came highly recommended. At the time, I was at a crossroads in my career and trying to determine my next steps. In advance of my session, I provided background information to the medium, like my full name, date of birth, my parents' full names, and my mother's maiden name. A few weeks later, we connected by telephone. For over an hour, he led me through an analysis of who I was and what I was supposed to be doing with my life. To say the session was provocative is an understatement. In the end, the main takeaway he provided was that my spirit guides advised, *you will need to write yourself out of your circumstances.* I was confounded by this conclusion and didn't know what that meant.

For years, I had aspired to write a novel. The first half of the story had already been penned in my head for years. But half of a story certainly doesn't qualify for a novel. Weeks after my psychic medium session, I was jarringly awakened in the middle of the night with a dream vision for the second half of the story. I was told what to write with such detail that it was eerie. But I didn't question it. I flipped off the bedcovers and attempted to slow my accelerated heartbeat. I hastily found pen and paper and furiously began making notes, desperately seeking to chronicle as much of the specificity and finer details that were revealed to me. I had never had anything like that happen, but I intuitively knew not to question it.

Over many months, I wrote and rewrote daily. I finally completed a draft of a novel in early 2011. Yet, I didn't feel like I was writing my way out of anything. Nothing tangible really changed from that writing experience. Or so I thought.

The second half of the story sets the protagonist on a spiritual and inspirational journey leading to mystical encounters across the American West with various strangers and places. Along the way, universal themes of love, loss, and grief, as well as Native American lore, are explored. Ultimately, the spiritual journey results in transformation and redemption.

*Why was I awakened in the middle of the night in 2010 with a clear and convincing message to write a story about grief, love, and redemption?* I asked myself over and over. Still, nothing revealed itself. The book sat idle, and no apparent change in my life occurred. After several years, I moved on and let go of the novel and message I had received.

Little did I know that nine short years later, I would suffer the most traumatic loss of my life and be compelled to confront profound grief, sorrow, and adversity on the deepest of personal levels. Now I understand why I was delivered that prescient message and told to write the story I ultimately penned. There is no comfort in that fact, but there's an understanding, which helps when seeking answers and healing your heart and soul.

The exercise of chronicling my grief after losing Jake and embarking on a migration from pain to purpose has been grueling yet necessary. As it turns out, I may have (finally) written myself out of the darkness of my circumstances and mustered the mettle to *walk on* in my life.

Thank you for taking the time to read *Walk On*. A portion of the proceeds from the sale of this book will directly support the two Jake Panus Walk On Scholarship funds.

To learn more, visit: *www.stephenpanus.com*

# Acknowledgments

TO MY WIFE, Kellie, I am grateful for your love and unconditional support, most especially during a time when neither of us knew up from down. We've stood together in the center of a fire, our bodies burned, bruised, and battered, our souls damaged and disfigured, yet we're still standing, loving, and living. I love you.

To Jake, my beloved son. While I still feel you in my heart and see you in my dreams, I deeply miss your physical presence, bear hugs, and the unadulterated joy you brought to everyone you encountered. The world is less brilliant without your smile, kindness, confidence, and laughter. Thank you for making me a better man, father, and husband. Until we see each other again.

To Liam, I offer you the words written by A.A. Milne and shared by Christopher Robin with Winnie the Pooh: "If ever there's a tomorrow when we're not together . . . you are braver than you believe, stronger than you seem, smarter than you think, and loved more than you'll ever know . . . but the most important thing is, even if we're ever apart, I will always be with you." I am so proud of the emotionally evolved young man you are. You are loved.

Thank you to John Koehler, Miranda Dillon, and everyone at Koehler Books who believed in me and my book and shared in the vision that I, through Jake, can make a positive difference in the lives of others. I appreciate all your patience, wisdom, and insights as you guided me through the publication process.

To Shane Beamer, thank you for taking the time and effort to write the preface. Shane may just be the most positive person I have ever encountered. He's one helluva football coach, an outstanding leader, and an even better person. I am proud to call Shane a good friend.

To my mother and late father, thank you for instilling such a positive outlook in me and forever nurturing it with love and support, no matter the circumstances.

To everyone who has and who continues to support the Jake Panus Walk On Scholarship funds, thank you so very much. Your generosity, love, and care for humanity are changing lives and fueling dreams.

To family, friends, and strangers who knowingly and unknowingly inspired me and encouraged me to follow the light amid the darkness, thank you.

Jake, 2019

Printed in Dunstable, United Kingdom